MW00851558

Block Buster QUILTS

I Love Nine Patches

16 Quilts from an All-Time Favorite Block

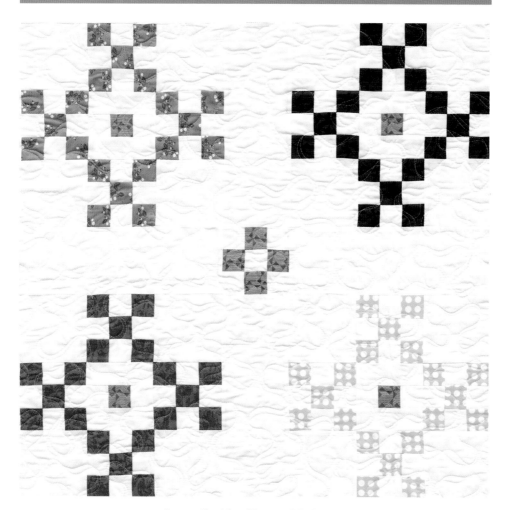

Compiled by Karen M. Burns

Martingale®
Create with Confidence

Block-Buster Quilts
I Love Nine Patches: 16 Quilts from an All-Time Favorite Block
© 2016 by Martingale & Company®

Martingale®
19021 120th Ave. NE, Ste. 102
Bothell, WA 98011-9511 USA
ShopMartingale.com

Printed in China
21 20 19 18 17 16   8 7 6 5 4 3 2 1

Library of Congress Cataloging-in-Publication Data
is available upon request.

ISBN: 978-1-60468-785-9

MISSION STATEMENT

We empower makers who use fabric and yarn
to make life more enjoyable.

CREDITS

**PUBLISHER AND
CHIEF VISIONARY OFFICER**
Jennifer Erbe Keltner

CONTENT DIRECTOR
Karen Costello Soltys

MANAGING EDITOR
Tina Cook

ACQUISITIONS EDITOR
Karen M. Burns

TECHNICAL WRITER
Beth Bradley

TECHNICAL EDITOR
Ellen Pahl

COPY EDITOR
Durby Peterson

DESIGN MANAGER
Adrienne Smitke

PRODUCTION MANAGER
Regina Girard

**COVER AND
INTERIOR DESIGNER**
Connor Chin

PHOTOGRAPHER
Brent Kane

ILLUSTRATOR
Lisa Lauch

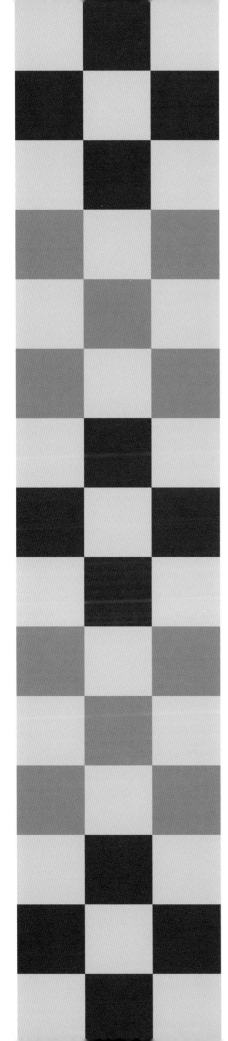

Contents

Introduction

Do you have a favorite memory about the quilts you've made or one you've wrapped up in? Quilting is more than just a hobby for many of us. It's a way of life, a way of making memories and commemorating special occasions, and a way of leaving a legacy for those we love. And when we think about making memorable quilts, it's often the timeless classics that come to mind—quilts that will be as well-loved generations from now as they are today.

Beginning with a classic block is one way to ensure a quilt pattern will stand the test of time. Few blocks have been around longer than the Nine Patch. Simple in its construction, it has many options for light and dark color placement, scrappy versus two-color, or even straight-set or on-point placement. For these reasons and many more, the Nine Patch block is an all-time favorite. That's why we've curated this collection of 16 quilts by top designers for you to enjoy.

Imagine the fun you'll have pairing your favorite Nine Patch patterns with special recipients in mind. Who knows, you might even choose one that's just right to wrap up in yourself. After all, Nine Patch blocks, quilting, and you—all three are worth celebrating!

Jennifer Keltner
Publisher and Chief Visionary Officer

Nine Patch Basics

Nine Patch blocks can be constructed from individual squares or by strip piecing, depending on the quilt pattern you're using. If you're using precut squares or scraps to construct the blocks, the individual-square method is your best bet, and chain piecing will speed up the process. On the other hand, if you want to create multiple Nine Patch blocks with identical fabric placement, strip piecing is an effective shortcut for constructing many units at once. Read on to learn both methods and add them to your Nine Patch repertoire.

Method 1: Chain Piecing Individual Squares

When making scrappy Nine Patch blocks, beginning with strip piecing doesn't allow for enough color variety. But sewing individual squares into blocks doesn't have to slow you down. Chain piecing makes the process quick and easy.

1. Cut or select five dark squares and four light squares. The featured block is composed of 2½" x 2½" squares that form a 6½" block **(fig. 1)**.

2. Flip the top-center square over the top-left square, so they are right sides together. Sew these squares together along the right edge; don't cut the thread. Continue by flipping the center square over the second square on the left. Stitch, and then continue sewing to join the bottom-center and left squares. Cut only the threads attached to the machine at the end of the stitching; don't cut the threads between the squares **(fig. 2)**. Press the seam allowances toward the darker fabric **(fig. 3)**.

3. Keeping the unit intact, sew the third square of the top row to the second square of that row; don't cut the thread. In the same way, join the third square of the middle row, and then the third square of the bottom row **(fig. 4)**. Cut only the last thread and press as before **(fig. 5)**.

4. Matching the seam intersections, sew the top row to the middle row **(fig. 6)**. Sew the middle row to the bottom row **(fig. 7)**. Press the seam allowances in one direction.

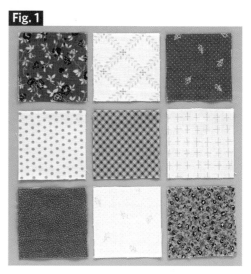

Fig. 1

Lay out squares in the desired arrangement.

Fig. 2

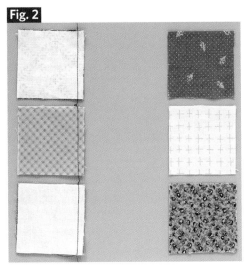

Sew the center column of squares to the squares on the left.

Fig. 3

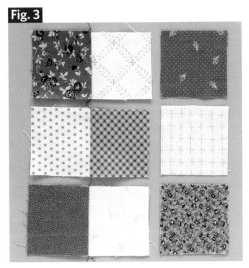

Keeping the units attached, press the seam allowances.

Fig. 4

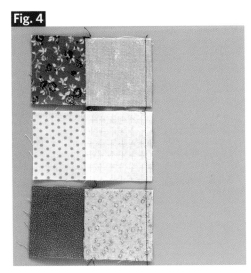

Sew the right column of squares to the center squares.

Fig. 5

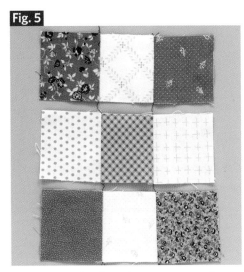

Keeping the threads intact, press the seam allowances.

Fig. 6

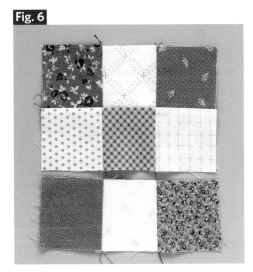

Join the top row to the center row, matching the seam intersections.

Fig. 7

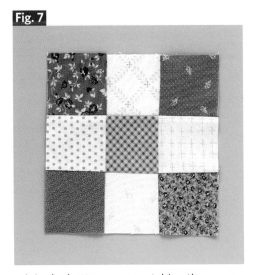

Join the bottom row, matching the seam intersections.

Method 2: Strip Piecing

This method saves time when cutting and sewing multiple units, making it ideal for quilts that require many matching Nine Patch blocks. Strip piecing also works well when using precut strips.

1. From the dark and light fabrics, cut three strips each. For the featured block, the strips are 2½" wide **(fig. 1)**.

2. Sew one light strip between two dark strips for strip set A. Sew the remaining dark strip between the two remaining light strips for strip set B **(fig. 2)**. Press the seam allowances toward the dark fabrics **(fig. 3).** When sewing long strips together, prevent the seams of the strip set from bowing or distorting by alternating the direction in which you sew them.

3. Trim off one end of the strip set to straighten the edge. Then crosscut two 2½"-wide segments from A. Cut one 2½"-wide segment from B **(fig. 4)**. Lay out the segments as shown **(fig. 5)**.

4. Matching the seam intersections, sew an A segment to the B segment. Sew the remaining A segment to the opposite side of the B segment **(fig. 6)**. Press the seam allowances in one direction or as indicated by the pattern.

5. As an alternative placement for the dark and light squares, use one A segment in the center of the block and two B segments for the sides **(fig. 7)**.

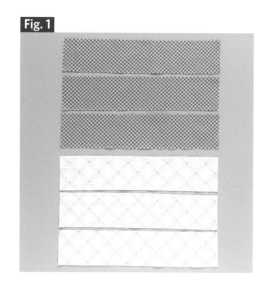

Fig. 1

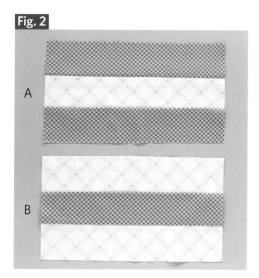

Fig. 2

A

B

Neat Seams

Maintaining a consistent seam allowance and pressing well are both key to sewing a neat and tidy Nine Patch block. Use a ¼" presser foot or mark the ¼" seam allowance on the bed of your machine with bright masking tape to serve as a guide. Thoroughly press seam allowances toward the darker fabric. When piecing the units, nest the seam allowances at the intersections by matching the seamlines and evenly distributing the seam-allowance bulk in opposite directions.

Fig. 3

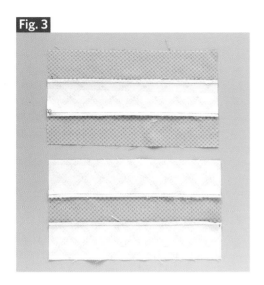

Fig. 6

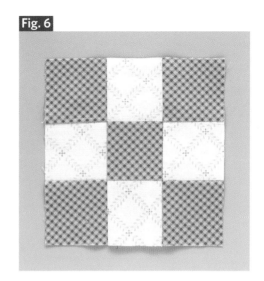

Fig. 4

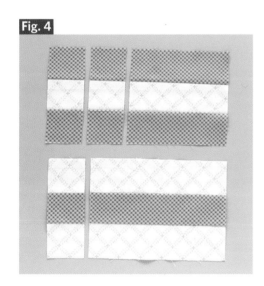

Fig. 7

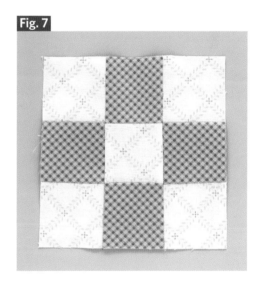

Fig. 5

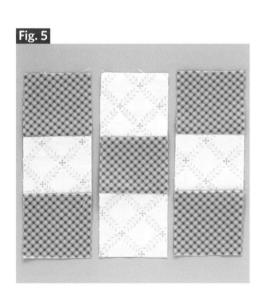

The Nine Patch block is very simple, but the grid of nine squares allows for a great deal of variation depending on the placement of colors or values (lights and darks) and scale of the pieces. The variety increases even more if you mix in half-square triangles or other pieced units as elements of the grid. Check out the following examples of alternative Nine Patch options and be inspired to design your own unique blocks.

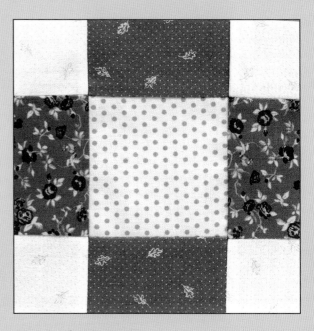

Plus Sign
Arrange the five dark squares in perpendicular rows crossing in the center of the block, and then place the four light squares in the corners to complete the grid. Or reverse the placement using five lights and four darks for the opposite effect.

Puss in the Corner
Vary the scale of the patches rather than using squares of identical sizes. The large center square is framed by narrow rectangles and small corner squares.

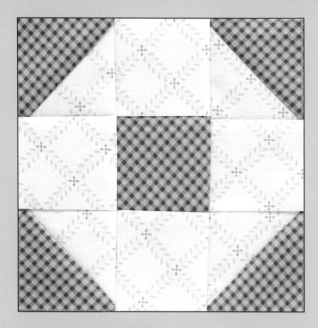

Single Wedding Ring

Incorporating half-square-triangle units adds a bit more complexity to the simple Nine Patch design. For this block, which Sherri McConnell also calls Snowball, place four half-square-triangle units in the corners of the grid, orienting them to form a continuous ring shape.

Double Nine Patch

For an intricate effect, make five small Nine Patch blocks for the corners and center unit of the grid. The small Nine Patch squares add strong diagonal lines to the block.

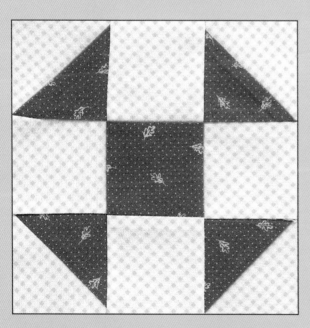

Shoo Fly

The Shoo Fly is a classic twist on the Nine Patch block. Place one dark square in the middle of the grid, and then place four half-square triangles in the corners, orienting the dark sides of the units toward the center.

Not So Plain, designed and pieced by Susan Ache; quilted by Carol Whitchurch

Finished quilt: 65½" x 85½"

Finished block: 5" x 5"

Not So Plain

*Q*uick and easy, this strip-pieced block is a simple variation of the classic Nine Patch; rather than nine squares, the block is divided unequally. One of the names for this block is Puss in the Corner. Another name is A Plain Block. Susan used a variety of prints and strips left over from other projects, which gives the quilt a look that's eclectic and scrappy—hence, not so plain!

Materials

Yardage is based on 42"-wide fabric. Fat quarters are approximately 18" x 21".

16 to 17 fat quarters OR 3¾ yards *total* of assorted light prints for blocks

16 to 17 fat quarters OR 3¾ yards *total* of assorted dark prints for blocks

⅔ yard of medium-value print for binding

5¼ yards of fabric for backing

74" x 94" piece of batting

Cutting

All measurements include ¼"-wide seam allowances. When cutting the fat quarters, be sure to cut across the 21" width, not the 18" length.

From the assorted light prints, cut:

37 strips, 3½" x 21"

74 strips, 1½" x 21"

From the assorted dark prints, cut:

37 strips, 3½" x 21"

74 strips, 1½" x 21"

From the medium-value print, cut:

8 strips, 2½" x 42"

Assembling the Blocks

1. Sew a light 3½" x 21" strip between two dark 1½" x 21" strips as shown. Press the seam allowances toward the dark strips. Make 37 strip sets. From *each* strip set, cut 6 A segments, 1½" wide, and 3 B segments, 3½" wide, for a total of 222 A segments and 111 B segments.

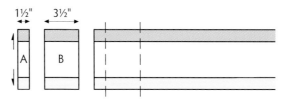

Make 37 strip sets.
From each, cut 6 of A and 3 of B.

2. Sew a dark 3½" x 21" strip between two light 1½" x 21" strips as shown. Press the seam allowances toward the dark strip. Make 37 strip sets. From *each* strip set, cut 6 C segments, 1½" wide, and 3 D segments, 3½" wide, for a total of 222 C segments and 111 D segments.

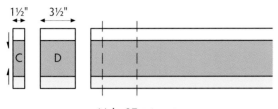

Make 37 strip sets.
From each, cut 6 of C and 3 of D.

3. Sew a D segment between two assorted A segments as shown. Press the seam allowances toward the D segment to make block A. Make 111 A blocks. The blocks should measure 5½" square.

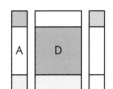

Block A.
Make 111.

4. Sew a B segment between two assorted C segments as shown. Press the seam allowances toward the C segments to make block B. Make 110 B blocks. You'll have one extra B and two extra C segments. The blocks should measure 5½" square.

I-4

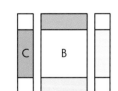 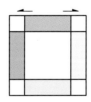

Block B.
Make 110.

Assembling the Quilt

1. Lay out seven A blocks and six B blocks in a row as shown. Join the blocks. Press the seam allowances toward the B blocks. Make nine rows.

Make 9.

2. Lay out seven B blocks and six A blocks in a row as shown. Join the blocks. Press the seam allowances toward the B blocks. Make eight rows.

Make 8.

3. Lay out the rows, alternating them as shown in the quilt assembly diagram. Join the rows; press the seam allowances in one direction.

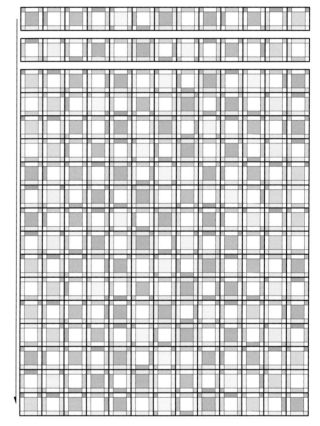

Quilt assembly

Finishing the Quilt

Go to ShopMartingale.com/HowtoQuilt for more details on quilting and finishing.

1. Layer the backing, batting, and quilt top; baste the layers together. Hand or machine quilt as desired. The quilt shown was quilted in an overall floral and swirl design, a nice complement to the straight lines of the blocks.

2. Use the medium-value 2½"-wide strips to make and attach the binding.

To the Nines

D iscover a classic Nine Patch quilt that offers a wonderful way to use up large scraps or dig into your stash and cut snippets from your favorite fabrics. The big, simple blocks are great for showcasing your treasured prints.

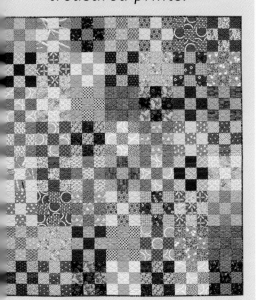

Materials

Yardage is based on 42"-wide fabric.

⅛ yard *each* of 56 bright prints for blocks

⅝ yard of gray print for binding

4 yards of fabric for backing

71" x 80" piece of batting

Cutting

All measurements include ¼"-wide seam allowances. Keep like prints together after cutting.

From *each* of the bright prints, cut:

    1 strip, 3½" x 42"; crosscut into 3 strips, 3½" x 12"

From the gray print, cut:

    7 strips, 2½" x 42"

Assembling the Blocks

1. Sort and choose fabric pairs for the blocks. Three strips *each* of two bright prints will make two Nine Patch blocks. You should have 28 pairs of bright prints.

2. Sew the strips from one fabric pair together to make two strip sets as shown. Press the seam allowances away from the center in strip set 1 and toward the center in strip set 2. Cut three segments, 3½" wide, from each strip set.

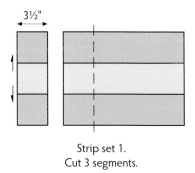

Strip set 1.
Cut 3 segments.

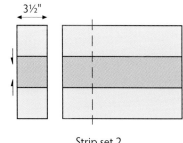

Strip set 2.
Cut 3 segments.

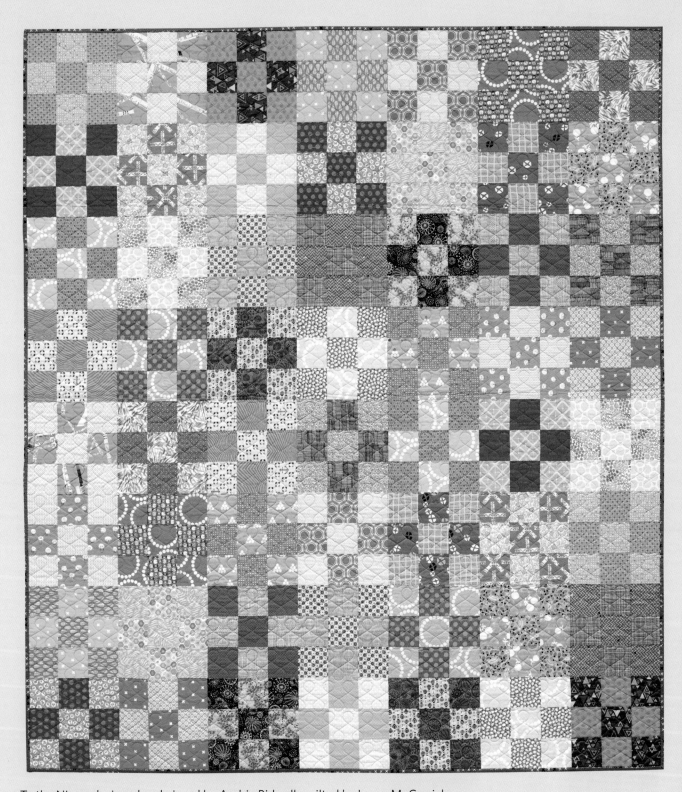

To the Nines, designed and pieced by Audrie Bidwell; quilted by Laura McCarrick

Finished quilt: 63½" x 72½"

Finished block: 9" x 9"

3. To make block A, sew one segment from strip set 2 between two segments from strip set 1 as shown. Press the seam allowances away from the center. To make block B, sew one segment from strip set 1 between two segments from strip set 2 as shown; press the seam allowances toward the center. The blocks should measure 9½" x 9½".

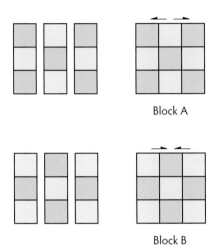

Block A

Block B

4. Repeat steps 2 and 3 to make one block A and one block B for each of the remaining fabric pairs. Make a total of 56 blocks.

Assembling the Quilt

Arrange the blocks in eight rows of seven blocks each, alternating the A and B blocks so the seams will nest together. Join the blocks in each row; press the seam allowances in opposite directions from row to row. Join the rows; press the seam allowances in one direction.

Finishing the Quilt

Go to ShopMartingale.com/HowtoQuilt for more details on quilting and finishing.

1. Layer the backing, batting, and quilt top; baste the layers together. Hand or machine quilt as desired. The quilt shown was machine quilted in an overall loop design.

2. Use the gray 2½"-wide strips to make and attach the binding.

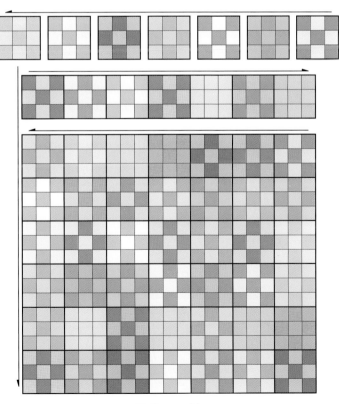

Quilt assembly

Lollipops by Barb Cherniwchan for Coach House Designs
Finished quilt: 61½" x 79½"
Finished block: 9" x 9"

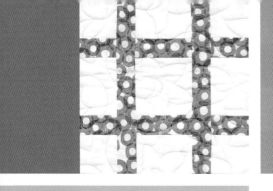

Lollipops

*A*dd narrow sashing within a Nine Patch block to create a pretty windowpane effect. Sweet lollipop appliqués frame the colorful center for a cheery touch.

Materials

Yardage is based on 42"-wide fabric.

3¼ yards of white tone on tone for blocks and middle border

⅜ yard *each* of gold, green, red, blue, and purple polka dot for blocks

1¼ yards of red tone on tone for appliqué, inner border, and binding

⅔ yard of red print for outer border

¼ yard of green tone on tone for appliqué

¼ yard of gold tone on tone for appliqué

⅛ yard of blue tone on tone for appliqué

5 yards of fabric for backing

68" x 86" piece of batting

Freezer paper for appliqué

Water-soluble basting glue

Cutting

All measurements include ¼"-wide seam allowances.

Prepare freezer-paper templates for the appliqués using the patterns on page 22 and referring to "Preparing the Appliqué" on page 21, or use your preferred appliqué method.

From the white tone on tone, cut:

7 strips, 5½" x 42"

13 strips, 3½" x 42"; crosscut into:

39 squares, 3½" x 3½"

140 rectangles, 2½" x 3½"

9 strips, 2½" x 42"; crosscut into 140 squares, 2½" x 2½"

From *each* of the polka dots, cut:

7 strips, 1½" x 42"; crosscut into:

14 rectangles, 1½" x 9½"

14 rectangles, 1½" x 3½"

28 rectangles, 1½" x 2½"

From the red tone on tone, cut:

8 strips, 1½" x 42"; crosscut *2 of the strips* into:

8 rectangles, 1½" x 5½"

8 rectangles, 1½" x 3½"

8 strips, 2½" x 42"

8 of appliqué A

12 of appliqué B

Continued on page 20

Continued from page 19

From the blue tone on tone, cut:

8 of appliqué A

From the gold tone on tone, cut:

12 of appliqué A

8 of appliqué B

From the green tone on tone, cut:

8 of appliqué B

24 of appliqué C

From the red print, cut:

7 strips, 2½" x 42"

Assembling the Blocks

1. To make the center unit, sew a white 3½" square between two red polka-dot 1½" x 3½" rectangles; press the seam allowances toward the red polka-dot rectangles. Sew white 2½" x 3½" rectangles to the red polka-dot rectangles at the top and bottom of the unit as shown; press. Sew red polka-dot 1½" x 9½" rectangles to the sides of the unit; press.

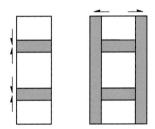

2. To make the side units, sew a white 2½" x 3½" rectangle between two red polka-dot 1½" x 2½" rectangles. Sew white 2½" x 2½" squares to the top and bottom of the unit. Repeat to make two side units.

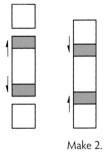

Make 2.

3. Sew the side units to the center unit as shown; press the seam allowances toward the side units. Make a total of seven red polka-dot blocks.

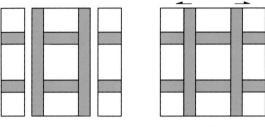

Make 7.

4. Repeat steps 1–3 with each polka-dot color to make 7 blocks of each color for a total of 35 blocks. The blocks should measure 9½" square. (You'll have four white 3½" squares left for the border.)

Assembling the Quilt Center

1. Arrange the blocks in seven rows of five blocks each, placing one block of each color per row as shown. Join the blocks in each row; press the seam allowances in alternate directions from row to row.

2. Join the rows; press the seam allowances in one direction. The quilt center should measure 45½" x 63½".

Quilt assembly

Preparing the Appliqué

1. Using the patterns on page 22, trace the appliqué shapes onto the dull side of the freezer paper. (Make multiple copies of the same template shape in order to work on several shapes at once.) Cut out the template along the drawn line. Using an iron, press the template shiny side down onto the right side of each appliqué fabric. Cut the fabric ⅛" to ¼" larger than the paper template.

2. Turn the template so the wrong side of the fabric is facing up. If necessary, snip the inner curves within one or two threads of the template so you can fold the fabric back along the template edge.

3. Apply a thin line of water-soluble basting glue along the extended fabric edge. Using your fingers, an awl, or the tip of a seam ripper, fold the fabric toward the wrong side, using the template edge as a guide. The short ends of the stem pieces will be hidden behind the circles, so it's not necessary to finish them.

4. Remove the freezer paper and reuse the template if possible. If any basting glue is visible on the right side of the appliqué, dab it away later with a damp cloth, after the appliqués are sewn to the quilt top.

Assembling the Borders

1. Sew the white 5½" x 42" strips together end to end using diagonal seams. From the total length, cut two 65½" side borders and two 47½" top and bottom borders.

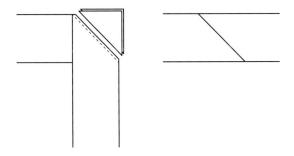

2. Refer to the photo on page 18 and the diagram on page 22 to position the appliqués on the white borders. Apply small dots of basting glue ¼" from the edge on the wrong side of the appliqué shapes, and then gently press the shapes in position on the borders. Stitch the appliqués in place by hand or machine using your preferred stitch.

3. Sew the six red 1½" x 42" strips together end to end using diagonal seams. From the total length, cut two 63½"-long side borders. Sew the borders to the sides of the quilt center; press the seam allowances toward the borders. From the remaining length, cut two 47½" borders for the top and bottom. Sew the borders to the top and bottom of the quilt center; press.

4. Sew red 1½" x 3½" rectangles to opposite sides of each remaining white 3½" square; press the seam allowances toward the red rectangles. Sew red 1½" x 5½" rectangles to the top and bottom of the squares; press.

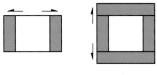

Make 4.

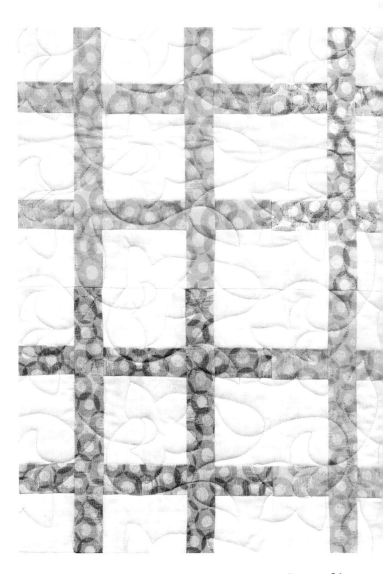

5. Sew the long appliquéd borders to the sides of the quilt top; press the seam allowances toward the red borders. Sew the corner squares to the ends of the short appliquéd borders, and then sew the top and bottom borders to the quilt top. Press the seam allowances toward the red borders.

6. Join the red-print 2½" x 42" strips end to end using a diagonal seam. Cut two 75½" lengths and sew them to the sides of the quilt top. Press the seam allowances toward the red borders. Cut two 61½" lengths and sew them to the top and bottom of the quilt top; press.

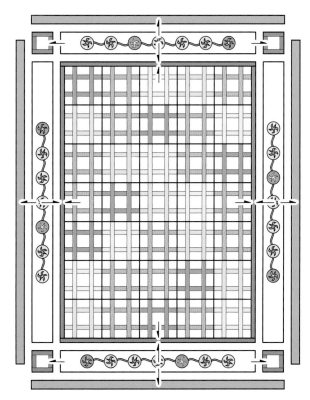

Adding borders

Finishing the Quilt

Go to ShopMartingale.com/HowtoQuilt for more details on quilting and finishing.

1. Layer the backing, batting, and quilt top; baste the layers together. Hand or machine quilt as desired. The quilt shown was machine quilted in an overall flower-and-leaf design using variegated thread in colors that coordinate with the fabric.

2. Use the red 2½"-wide strips to make and attach the binding.

Appliqué patterns do not include seam allowances.

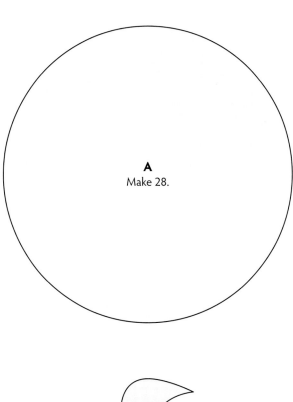

A
Make 28.

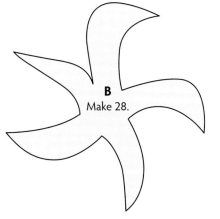

B
Make 28.

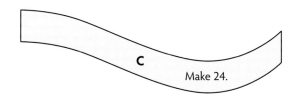

C
Make 24.

Bespoke

*E*njoy using a combination of half-square-triangle units and four-patch units to create two Nine Patch block variations. The block combination makes this charming quilt much easier to piece than it looks!

Materials

Yardage is based on 42"-wide fabric.

3 yards of white solid for blocks

¼ yard *each* of 12 assorted bright prints for Star blocks

1 yard of gray polka dot for Chain blocks

⅝ yard of aqua-and-white stripe for binding

3⅞ yards of fabric for backing

68" x 80" piece of batting

Cutting

All measurements include ¼"-wide seam allowances.

From the white solid, cut:

8 strips, 5" x 42"; crosscut into 60 squares, 5" x 5"

8 strips, 2½" x 42"

8 strips, 4½" x 42"; crosscut into 60 squares, 4½" x 4½"

From *each* of the assorted bright prints, cut:

1 strip, 5" x 42"; crosscut into:

5 squares, 5" x 5" (60 total)

1 square, 4½" x 4½" (12 total)

From the remainder of the bright-print strips, cut *a total of:*

3 squares, 4½" x 4½"

From the gray polka dot, cut:

8 strips, 2½" x 42"

2 strips, 4½" x 42"; crosscut into 15 squares, 4½" x 4½"

From the aqua-and-white stripe, cut:

7 strips, 2½" x 42"

Bespoke, designed by Corey Yoder; quilted by Abby Latimer

Finished quilt: 60½" x 72½"

Finished block: 12" x 12"

Assembling the Star Blocks

1. Draw a diagonal line from corner to corner on the wrong side of each white 5" square.

2. With right sides together, place a marked white square on top of a print 5" square. Sew ¼" from each side of the drawn line. Cut along the drawn line to yield two half-square-triangle units. Press the seam allowances toward the print, and then trim the units to 4½" square. Make 120 units.

Make 120.

3. Lay out eight assorted half-square-triangle units and one print 4½" square in three rows as shown. Join the units in each row; press the seam allowances as indicated. Join the rows; press the seam allowances away from the center row. Make 15 blocks, which should measure 12½" square.

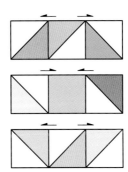 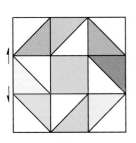

Make 15.

Assembling the Chain Blocks

1. Join one gray 2½" x 42" strip and one white 2½" x 42" strip to create a strip set. Press the seam allowances toward the gray strip. Make eight strip sets. Crosscut the strip sets into 120 segments, 2½" wide.

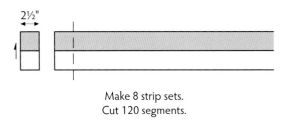

Make 8 strip sets.
Cut 120 segments.

2. Join two segments as shown to make a four-patch unit measuring 4½" x 4½". Press. Make 60 units.

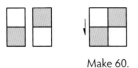

Make 60.

3. Lay out four of the four-patch units, four white 4½" squares, and one gray 4½" square. Join the units in each row; press as indicated. Join the rows; press the seam allowances toward the center. Make 15 blocks, which should measure 12½" square.

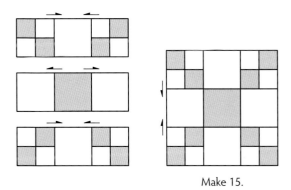

Make 15.

Assembling the Quilt

Arrange the blocks in six rows of five blocks each, alternating the blocks as shown in the quilt assembly diagram. Join the blocks in each row; press the seam allowances toward the Chain blocks. Join the rows; press the seam allowances in one direction.

Finishing the Quilt

Go to ShopMartingale.com/HowtoQuilt for more details on quilting and finishing.

1. Layer the backing, batting, and quilt top; baste the layers together. Hand or machine quilt as desired. The quilt shown was machine quilted in an overall spiral design.

2. Use the aqua-and-white 2½" strips to make and attach the binding.

Quilt assembly

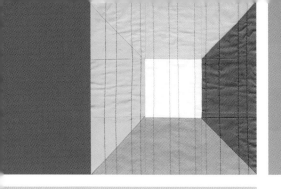

Jewel of the Nine

The clever mix of the two Nine Patch blocks creates a faceted, dimensional effect. Use vibrant solids and prints to bring to mind shimmering jewels.

Materials

Yardage is based on 42"-wide fabric.

¼ yard *each* of 8 assorted bright prints for blocks

½ yard *each* of pink, light-blue, orange, green, and yellow solid for blocks

1⅛ yards of purple solid for blocks, border, and binding

½ yard of dark-pink solid for blocks and border

¼ yard of dark-blue solid for blocks

¼ yard of white solid for blocks

3⅝ yards of fabric for backing

65" x 74" piece of batting

Cutting

All measurements include ¼"-wide seam allowances.

From *each* of the 8 assorted bright prints, cut:

2 strips, 3½" x 42" (16 total)

From the dark-pink solid, cut:

2 strips, 3½" x 42"

3 strips, 1½" x 42"

From the pink solid, cut:

12 squares, 3⅞" x 3⅞"; cut in half diagonally to yield 24 triangles

12 squares, 3½" x 3½"

From the light-blue solid, cut:

14 squares, 3⅞" x 3⅞"; cut in half diagonally to yield 28 triangles

14 squares, 3½" x 3½"

From the orange solid, cut:

11 squares, 3⅞" x 3⅞"; cut in half diagonally to yield 22 triangles

11 squares, 3½" x 3½"

From the green solid, cut:

15 squares, 3⅞" x 3⅞"; cut in half diagonally to yield 30 triangles

15 squares, 3½" x 3½"

From the yellow solid, cut:

12 squares, 3⅞" x 3⅞"; cut in half diagonally to yield 24 triangles

12 squares, 3½" x 3½"

Continued on page 29

Jewel of the Nine by Jackie White

Finished quilt: 56½" x 65½"

Finished block: 9" x 9"

Continued from page 27

From the purple solid, cut:

11 squares, 3⅞" x 3⅞"; cut in half diagonally to yield 22 triangles

15 squares, 3½" x 3½"

3 strips, 1½" x 42"

7 strips, 2½" x 42"

From the dark-blue solid, cut:

7 squares, 3⅞" x 3⅞"; cut in half diagonally to yield 14 triangles

7 squares, 3½" x 3½"

From the white solid, cut:

21 squares, 3½" x 3½"

Assembling the A Blocks

1. Sew three different print 3½" x 42" strips together along the long edges to make a strip set; press the seam allowances away from the center. Make two matching strip sets. Repeat, using three different prints, to make another pair of matching strip sets. Crosscut each strip set into 11 segments, 3½" wide, for a total of 44. (Two will be extra).

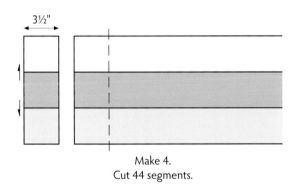

3½"

Make 4.
Cut 44 segments.

2. Sew a dark-pink 3½" x 42" strip between two different print 3½" x 42" strips to make a strip set; press the seam allowances toward the dark-pink strip. Make two strip sets. Crosscut each strip set into 11 segments, 3½" wide, for a total of 22. (One will be extra).

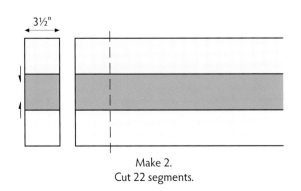

3½"

Make 2.
Cut 22 segments.

3. Lay out two print segments and one dark-pink segment with the dark pink in the middle as shown. Join the units and press the seam allowances away from the center. Repeat to make 21 of block A, which should measure 9½" square.

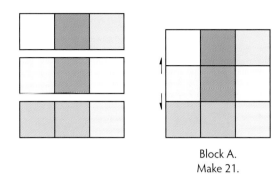

Block A.
Make 21.

Assembling the B Blocks

1. Sew the solid 3⅞" triangles together along the diagonal edges to create half-square-triangle units in the combinations and quantities shown. Press the seam allowances toward the darker fabric.

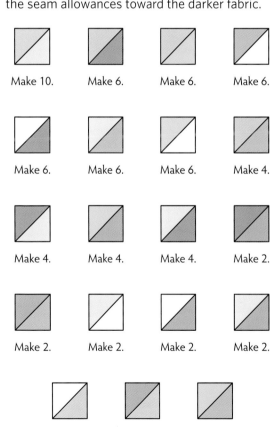

Make 10.   Make 6.   Make 6.   Make 6.

Make 6.   Make 6.   Make 6.   Make 4.

Make 4.   Make 4.   Make 4.   Make 2.

Make 2.   Make 2.   Make 2.   Make 2.

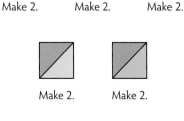

Make 2.   Make 2.   Make 2.

Make 2.   Make 2.

2. Lay out four half-square-triangle units, four solid 3½" squares, and one white 3½" square in rows as shown. Join the units in each row; press the seam allowances as indicated. Join the rows; press the seam allowances toward the center.

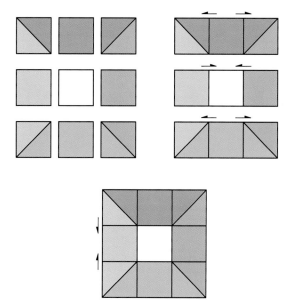

Block B.
Make 21.

3. Repeat step 2 to assemble the remaining 20 blocks in the combinations shown using the solid squares and half-square-triangle units. You'll have a total of 21 B blocks, which should measure 9½" square.

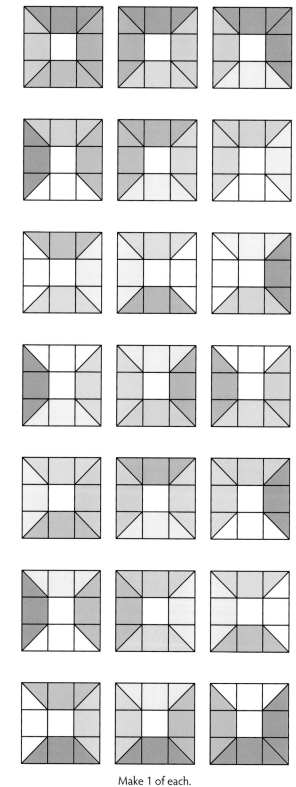

Make 1 of each.

Assembling the Quilt

1. Lay out the blocks according to the quilt assembly diagram, paying close attention to the placement and orientation of the B blocks in order to form the pattern of colors surrounding the A blocks. Join the blocks in each row; press the seam allowances in alternate directions from row to row. Join the rows; press the seam allowances in one direction.

2. Join the dark-pink 1½" x 42" strips end to end. Repeat to join the purple 1½" x 42" strips. Cut one pink and one purple 1½" x 63½" strip for the side borders. Sew the purple strip to the left side of the quilt and the pink strip to the right side; press the seam allowances toward the border strips. Cut one pink and one purple 56½"-long strip; sew the pink strip to the top and the purple strip to the bottom of the quilt; press.

Finishing the Quilt

Go to ShopMartingale.com/HowtoQuilt for more details on quilting and finishing.

1. Layer the backing, batting, and quilt top; baste the layers together. Hand or machine quilt as desired. The quilt shown was machine quilted in vertical parallel lines using pink, purple, yellow, green, and blue thread.

2. Use the purple 2½"-wide strips to make and attach the binding.

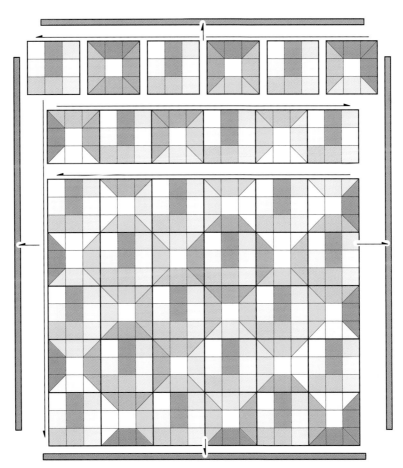

Quilt assembly

Dew Drops, designed by Kari M. Carr of New Leaf Stitches; quilted by Penny Miller
Fabric courtesy of Adornit Fabrics; sewn on a Bernina 970

Finished quilt: 46½" x 58½"

Finished block: 9" x 9"

Dew Drops

*S*erene and peaceful as the morning dew, this Nine Patch design is all about sweetness and movement. With the pairing of eye-catching blocks and sashing, it's easy to overlook that this block's construction is really a variation on a basic Nine Patch made with not-so-basic units.

Materials

Yardage is based on 42"-wide fabric.

1½ yards of aqua print for outer border

1¼ yards of cream tone on tone for background

⅝ yard of black print for inner border

⅝ yard of yellow print for blocks and binding

½ yard of turquoise print for blocks

¼ yard of pink print for diamonds

3 yards of fabric for backing

54" x 66" piece of batting

Template plastic or Tri-Recs tools*

*Tri-Recs tools by EZ Quilting are available at quilt shops and online.

Cutting

All measurements include ¼"-wide seam allowances. If you do not have the Tri-Recs tools, make templates for the side and center triangles using the patterns on page 36. To cut the mirror-image side triangles, see the illustration on page 34.

From the turquoise print, cut:

2 strips, 4" x 42"; crosscut into 12 squares, 4" x 4"

2 strips, 3½" x 42"; crosscut into 24 pairs of mirror-image side triangles

From the cream tone on tone, cut:

2 strips, 4" x 42"; crosscut into 12 squares, 4" x 4"

6 strips, 3½" x 42"; crosscut into:

18 squares, 3½" x 3½"

8 rectangles, 3½" x 6½"

4 rectangles, 3½" x 9½"

24 center triangles

4 strips, 2" x 42"; crosscut into 68 squares, 2" x 2"

From the yellow print, cut:

1 strip, 3½" x 42"; crosscut into 6 squares, 3½" x 3½"

6 strips, 2½" x 42"

From the pink print, cut:

2 strips, 3½" x 42"; crosscut into 21 squares, 3½" x 3½"

Continued on page 34

Continued from page 33

From the black print, cut:

1 strip, 2" x 42"; crosscut into 16 squares, 2" x 2"

4 strips, 3½" x 42"; crosscut into:

2 strips, 3½" x 39½"

6 rectangles, 3½" x 9½"

From the aqua print, cut *on the lengthwise grain:*

2 strips, 7" x 45½"

2 strips, 7" x 46½"

Assembling the Blocks

1. To cut the side triangles, keep the turquoise strips folded in half so they are 3½" x 21". Place the template or Tri-Recs ruler on the fabric to mark and cut one pair of mirror-image triangles. Reverse the placement of the template/tool and cut another pair as shown. Cut 24 pairs total.

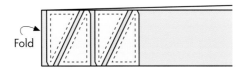

2. With right sides together, stitch a turquoise left-side triangle to the left edge of a cream center triangle as shown. Press the seam allowances open. Sew a right-side triangle to the right edge of the center triangle; press. The unit should measure 3½" square. Make 24 units.

Make 24.

3. Draw a diagonal line from corner to corner on the wrong side of the cream 4" squares. With right sides together, place a marked square on a turquoise 4" square. Stitch ¼" from each side of the drawn line. Cut along the line to yield 2 half-square-triangle units. Press the seam allowances open. Trim to 3½" square. Make 24 units.

Make 24.

4. Lay out four units from step 2, four half-square-triangle units, and one yellow 3½" square in three rows as shown. Join the units in each row; press the seam allowances as indicated. Join the rows; press the seam allowances toward the center. The block should measure 9½" square. Make six blocks.

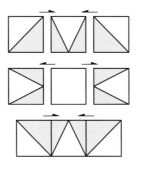 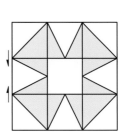

Make 6.

Assembling the Sashing and Inner Border

1. Draw a diagonal line from corner to corner on the wrong side of the cream 2" squares.

2. With right sides together, place marked squares on opposite corners of a pink 3½" square. Stitch along the drawn lines and trim the seam allowances to ¼". Press the seam allowances toward the corners. Repeat the process to stitch squares to the remaining corners. Make 17 pink-and-cream diamond units, which should measure 3½" square.

Make 17.

3. Sew cream 3½" squares to opposite sides of a pink-and-cream diamond unit. Press the seam allowances open. Make nine vertical sashing units.

Make 9.

4. Join three sashing units and two blocks as shown. Press the seam allowances open. Make three rows.

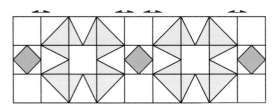

Make 3.

5. Join two pink-and-cream diamond units, two cream 3½" x 6½" rectangles, and one cream 3½" x 9½" rectangle as shown. Press the seam allowances open. Make four horizontal sashing strips.

Make 4.

6. Repeat steps 1 and 2 using the black 2" squares and the remaining pink 3½" squares to make four pink-and-black diamond units.

Make 4.

7. Join two pink-and-black diamond units and three black 3½" x 9½" rectangles as shown. Press the seam allowances open. Make two strips for the top and bottom inner borders.

Make 2.

Assembling the Quilt

1. Join the sashing strips and block rows as shown in the quilt assembly diagram; press the seam allowances open.

2. Sew the black 3½" x 39½" strips to the sides of the quilt and press the seam allowances open. Sew the black pieced inner-border strips to the top and bottom; press.

3. Join the aqua 7" x 45½" strips to the sides of the quilt; press the seam allowances open or toward the aqua borders. Join the aqua 7" x 46½" strips to the top and bottom of the quilt; press.

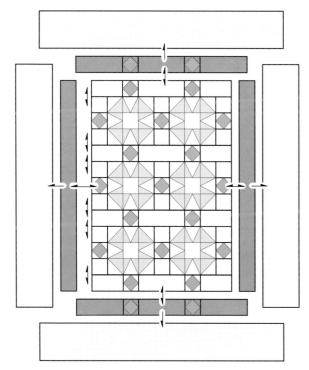

Quilt assembly

Finishing the Quilt

Go to ShopMartingale.com/HowtoQuilt for more details on quilting and finishing.

1. Layer the backing, batting, and quilt top; baste the layers together. Hand or machine quilt as desired. The featured quilt was machine quilted with a variety of shapes to highlight the design. There is a swirl-and-paisley pattern in the cream background, echo quilting in the diamonds and triangles, a triangular pattern in the black borders, and a feather and pebble pattern in the aqua border.

2. Use the yellow 2½"-wide strips to make and attach the binding.

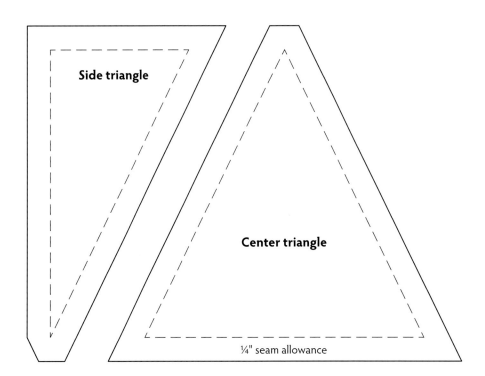

Side triangle

Center triangle

¼" seam allowance

Pretty in Plaid

*P*laid is a classic pattern no matter what the season, from fresh-and-sunny ginghams in summer to bold-and-rich buffalo plaids in fall. Because the Nine Patch blocks in this design lend themselves so well to quick construction methods, you can make the quilt time and again in a variety of favorite color palettes.

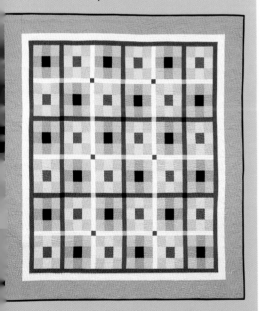

Materials

Yardage is based on 42"-wide fabric.

1⅓ yards of light-gray solid for blocks and sashing squares

1⅓ yards of medium-gray solid for outer border and sashing squares

1 yard of white tone on tone for sashing and middle border

⅞ yard of dark-gray solid for sashing, sashing squares, and inner border

⅞ yard of black solid for blocks, sashing squares, and binding

⅔ yard of light-pink solid for blocks

⅔ yard of medium-pink solid for blocks

¼ yard of dark-pink solid for blocks

5 yards of fabric for backing

76" x 85" piece of batting

Color Cues

It's important that the color values (darkness or lightness of the fabrics) vary enough from one another to be noticeable in the quilt. Each fabric manufacturer has unique names for solids, so it may take some comparison to find the right shades or tints.

The darkest color, identified here as black, may also be called *charcoal, coal,* or *graphite.* For the dark gray, consider fabric called *medium gray, titanium,* or possibly *steel.* The medium gray should be two or three shades lighter than the dark gray; it might go by the name *ash, smoke gray,* or *shadow.* For the light gray, look for fabric called *cloud gray, silver,* or *oyster shell.* It should be about two shades darker than the white tone-on-tone fabric.

Find a fabric named *dark rose pink* or *peony* for the dark pink. For the medium pink, the manufacturer may refer to the color as *'30s pink.* For the light pink, look for the name *pale pink, baby pink, blush,* or *light rose.* As with all colors, some pinks may look more blue or lavender (cool) or more coral or peach (warm), so lay the fabrics next to one another. If one looks more orange or blue next to the others, choose another with the same value but in a more compatible hue.

Pretty in Plaid, designed and pieced by Kari Ramsay; quilted by Wendy Nabhan

Finished quilt: 68¼" x 77¼"

Finished block: 7½" x 9"

Cutting

All measurements include ¼"-wide seam allowances.

From the light-gray solid, cut:

12 strips, 3½" x 42"; crosscut into 144 rectangles, 3" x 3½"

4 squares, 1¾" x 1¾"

From the light-pink solid, cut:

6 strips, 3½" x 42"; crosscut into 72 rectangles, 3" x 3½"

From the dark-pink solid, cut:

2 strips, 3½" x 42"; crosscut into 18 rectangles, 3" x 3½"

From the medium-pink solid, cut:

6 strips, 3½" x 42"; crosscut into 72 rectangles, 3" x 3½"

From the black solid, cut:

2 strips, 3½" x 42"; crosscut into 18 rectangles, 3" x 3½"

6 squares, 1¾" x 1¾"

8 strips, 2½" x 42"

From the dark-gray solid, cut:

14 strips, 1¾" x 42"; crosscut *8 of the strips* into:

12 strips, 1¾" x 8"

18 strips, 1¾" x 9½"

6 squares, 1¾" x 1¾"

From the white tone on tone, cut:

7 strips, 1¾" x 42"; crosscut into:

18 strips, 1¾" x 8"

12 strips, 1¾" x 9½"

6 strips, 2½" x 42"

From the medium-gray solid, cut:

9 squares, 1¾" x 1¾"

7 strips, 5½" x 42"

Assembling the Blocks

1. Lay out four light-gray 3" x 3½" rectangles, four light-pink 3" x 3½" rectangles, and one dark-pink 3" x 3½" rectangle as shown above right. Join the rectangles in each row; press the seam allowances of the top and bottom rows toward the light-gray rectangles and press the seam allowances of the center row toward the dark-pink rectangle. Join the rows; press the seam allowances toward the center row. Make 18 blocks with pink centers.

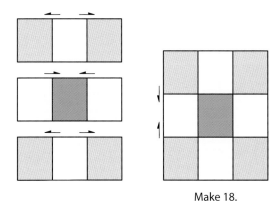

Make 18.

2. Lay out four light-gray 3" x 3½" rectangles, four medium-pink 3" x 3½" rectangles, and one black 3" x 3½" rectangle. Assemble the block in the same manner as the blocks with pink centers. Make 18 blocks with black centers.

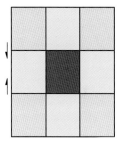

Make 18.

Assembling the Sashing

1. Sew a dark-gray 1¾" x 8" rectangle to the bottom of six blocks with pink centers. Sew a white 1¾" x 8" rectangle to the bottom of nine blocks with pink centers. Press the seam allowances toward the rectangles just added. Set aside the remaining three blocks with pink centers.

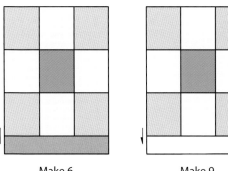

Make 6. Make 9.

2. Sew a dark-gray 1¾" x 8" rectangle to the bottom of six blocks with black centers. Sew a white 1¾" x 8" rectangle to the bottom of nine blocks with black centers. Press the seam allowances toward the rectangles just added. Set aside the remaining three blocks with black centers.

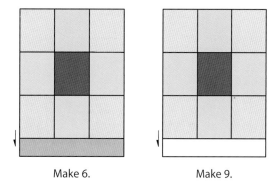

Make 6.   Make 9.

3. Sew six dark-gray 1¾" x 9½" rectangles, three medium-gray 1¾" squares, and two black 1¾" squares together as shown. Press the seam allowances toward the rectangles. Make three rows.

Make 3.

4. Sew six white 1¾" x 9½" rectangles, three dark-gray 1¾" squares, and two light-gray 1¾" squares together as shown; press the seam allowances toward the rectangles. Make two rows.

Make 2.

Assembling the Quilt

1. Lay out the blocks and sashing in columns as shown in the quilt assembly diagram above right. Join the blocks in each column; press the seam allowances toward the sashing rectangles. Join the columns to the adjacent vertical sashing; press the

seam allowances toward the vertical sashing. The quilt top should measure 51¾" x 60¾".

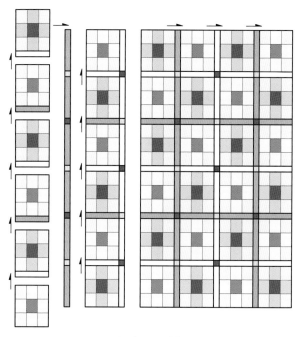

Quilt assembly

2. Join the six dark-gray 1¾" x 42" strips end to end for the inner border. Measure the quilt top vertically through the center. From the total length, cut two strips to that measurement for the side borders. Sew the borders to the sides of the quilt; press the seam allowances toward the borders. Measure the quilt top horizontally through the center, including the borders just added. Cut two strips to that measurement and sew the borders to the top and bottom of the quilt; press.

3. Repeat step 2 using the white 2½" x 42" strips to make and attach the middle border.

4. Repeat step 2 using the medium-gray 5½" x 42" strips to make and attach the outer border.

Finishing the Quilt

Go to ShopMartingale.com/HowtoQuilt for more details on quilting and finishing.

1. Layer the backing, batting, and quilt top; baste the layers together. Hand or machine quilt as desired. The quilt shown was machine quilted in an echoing diamond pattern.

2. Use the black 2½"-wide strips to make and attach the binding.

Take a Bite out of Life

*Y*ou can add an asymmetrical touch to a basic Nine Patch block for an unexpected composition. Using a square of background fabric gives these blocks their "bite."

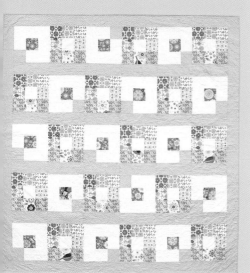

Materials

Yardage is based on 42"-wide fabric. Fat quarters are approximately 18" x 21".

2⅛ yards of light-gray solid for blocks, sashing, border, and binding

8 fat quarters of assorted bright prints for blocks

1½ yards of white solid for blocks

¼ yard of dark-pink print for blocks

3⅞ yards of fabric for backing

69" x 72" piece of batting

Cutting

All measurements include ¼"-wide seam allowances. When cutting fat quarters, be sure to cut across the 21" width, not the 18" length.

From the dark-pink print, cut:

2 strips, 3½" x 42"

From the white solid, cut:

2 strips, 6½" x 42"

10 strips, 3½" x 42; crosscut *6 of the strips* into:

15 rectangles, 3½" x 9½"

15 squares, 3½" x 3½"

From the light-gray solid, cut:

14 strips, 3½" x 42"; crosscut *6 of the strips* into 24 rectangles, 3½" x 9½"

7 strips, 2½" x 42"

From *each* of the assorted bright prints, cut:

3 strips, 3½" x 21"; crosscut into 15 squares, 3½" x 3½" (120 squares total)

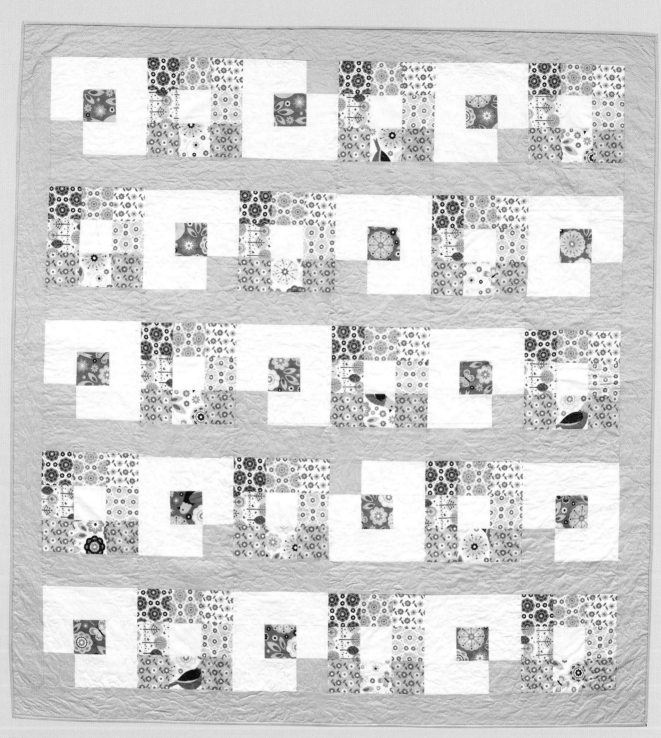

Take a Bite out of Life by Jackie White
Finished quilt: 60½" x 63½"
Finished block: 9" x 9"

Assembling the A Blocks

1. Sew a dark-pink 3½" x 42" strip between two white 3½" x 42" strips as shown. Press the seam allowances toward the pink strip. Make two strip sets. From the two strip sets, cut a total of 15 segments, 3½" wide.

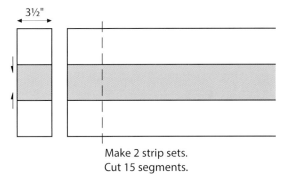

Make 2 strip sets.
Cut 15 segments.

2. Sew a white 6½" x 42" strip to a gray 3½" x 42" strip as shown. Press the seam allowances toward the gray strip. Make two strip sets. From the two strip sets, cut a total of 15 segments, 3½" wide.

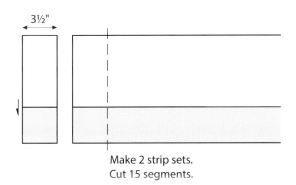

Make 2 strip sets.
Cut 15 segments.

3. Lay out one segment from step 1 for the center row, one segment from step 2 for the top row, and one white 3½" x 9½" rectangle for the bottom row as shown. Join the rows to complete block A. Press the seam allowances in one direction. Make 15 A blocks, which should measure 9½" square.

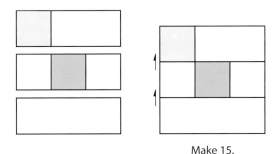

Make 15.

Assembling the B Blocks

1. Sew a white 3½" square between two bright-print 3½" squares to make a row. Press the seam allowances toward the print squares. Make 15 rows.

Make 15.

2. Sew three bright-print 3½" squares together to make a row. Press the seam allowances toward the center square. Make 30 rows.

Make 30.

3. Sew two bright-print rows from step 2 and one row from step 1 together with the white square in the center as shown. Press the seam allowances in one direction. Make 15 B blocks.

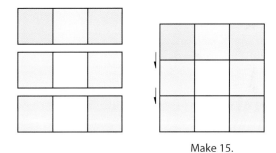

Make 15.

Custom Composition

Jackie arranged the "Bite" blocks (Block A) to her liking in the featured quilt, but feel free to rotate them as you wish in your quilt top to create a different composition.

Assembling the Quilt

1. Arrange the blocks in five rows of six blocks each, alternating A and B blocks as shown below. Rotate the A blocks as desired or according to the quilt assembly diagram. Sew a gray 3½" x 9½" rectangle to the bottom of the blocks in every row except those in the bottom row. Press the seam allowances toward the gray rectangles.

2. Join the blocks in each row; press the seam allowances in alternate directions from row to row. Join the rows; press the seam allowances in one direction.

3. Join the remaining gray 3½" x 42" strips end to end. Cut two strips, 57½" long, and sew them to the sides of the quilt. Press the seam allowances toward the borders. Cut two strips, 60½" long, and sew them to the top and bottom of the quilt; press.

Finishing the Quilt

Go to ShopMartingale.com/HowtoQuilt for more details on quilting and finishing.

1. Layer the backing, batting, and quilt top; baste the layers together. Hand or machine quilt as desired. The quilt shown was machine quilted with an allover loop design.

2. Use the gray 2½"-wide strips to make and attach the binding.

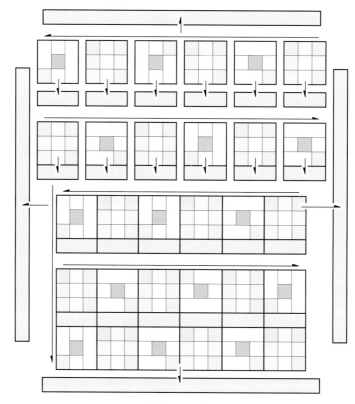

Quilt assembly

Gradations

*P*lay with scale using three different sizes of Nine Patch blocks to create a gradated effect across the quilt. For maximum graphic impact, use cheerful prints and a bright-white background.

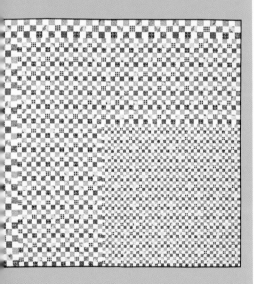

Materials

Yardage is based on 42"-wide fabric.

5 yards of white solid for blocks

⅝ yard *each* of 4 assorted pink prints for blocks

⅝ yard *each* of 3 assorted blue prints for blocks

⅝ yard *each* of 2 green prints for blocks

¾ yard of dark-blue tone on tone for binding

7⅜ yards of fabric for backing

87" x 87" piece of batting

Cutting

All measurements include ¼"-wide seam allowances.

From the white solid, cut:

9 strips, 2½" x 42"

36 strips, 2" x 42"

45 strips, 1½" x 42"

From *each* of the assorted pink, blue, and green prints, cut:

1 strip, 2½" x 42" (9 total)

4 strips, 2" x 42" (36 total)

5 strips, 1½" x 42" (45 total)

From the dark-blue tone on tone, cut:

9 strips, 2½" x 42"

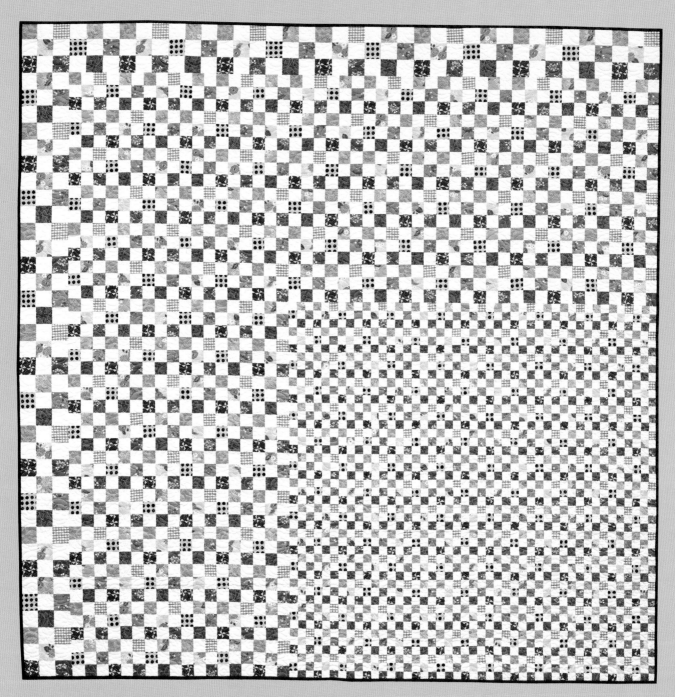

Gradations, designed and pieced by Kimberly Jolly; quilted by MyLongArm.com

Finished quilt: 78½" x 78½"

Finished blocks: 6" x 6", 4½" x 4½", and 3" x 3"

Assembling the Blocks

1. Sew a white 2½" x 42" strip between a pink 2½" x 42" strip and a blue 2½" x 42" strip as shown; press the seam allowances toward the print strips. Repeat to make the following strip sets from 2½" x 42" strips as shown:
   - 1 blue and 2 white strips
   - 1 white, 1 green, and 1 pink strip

   Cut 13 segments, 2½" wide, from each strip set.

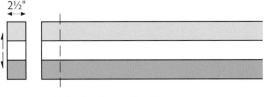

Make 1 strip set. Cut 13 segments.

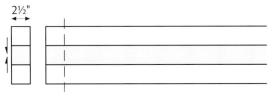

Make 1 strip set. Cut 13 segments.

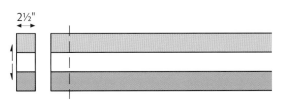

Make 1 strip set. Cut 13 segments.

2. Join the segments from step 1 as shown to make a Nine Patch block, 6½" square. Make 13 blocks.

 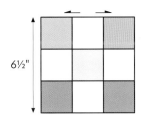

Make 13.

3. Make the following strip sets from 2½" x 42" strips:
   - 1 blue and 2 white strips
   - 1 white and 2 pink strips
   - 1 green and 2 white strips

   Cut 12 segments, 2½" wide, from each strip set.

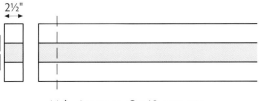

Make 1 strip set. Cut 12 segments.

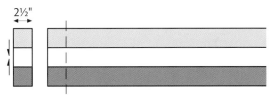

Make 1 strip set. Cut 12 segments.

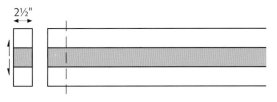

Make 1 strip set. Cut 12 segments.

4. Join the segments to make 12 Nine Patch blocks, 6½" square.

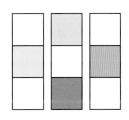 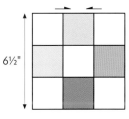

Make 12.

5. Repeat step 1 to make four strip sets of each color combination using the 2" x 42" strips. From each color combination, cut a total of 78 segments, 2" wide. Join one unit of each color combination as shown to make a 5" square Nine Patch block. Make 78 blocks.

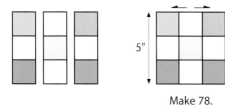

Make 78.

6. Repeat step 3 to make four strip sets of each color combination using the remaining 2" x 42" strips. From each color combination, cut a total of 78 segments, 2" wide. Join one unit of each color combination as shown to make a Nine Patch block, 5" square. Make 78 blocks.

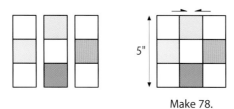

Make 78.

7. Repeat step 1 to make five strip sets of each color combination using the 1½" x 42" strips. Cut 113 segments, 1½" wide, from each color combination. Join the units to make 113 blocks, 3½" x 3½", as shown. Repeat step 3 to make five strip sets of each color combination using the remaining 1½" x 42" strips. Cut 112 segments, 1½" wide, and then join them to make 112 blocks.

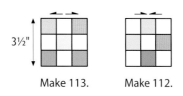

Make 113.   Make 112.

Assembling the Quilt

1. Arrange the 3½" blocks in a square grid, 15 rows of 15 blocks each, as shown in the quilt assembly diagram. Join the blocks in each row; press the seam allowances in alternate directions from row to row. Join the rows; press the seam allowances in one direction.

2. Arrange the 5" blocks in two sections, one with 10 rows of 6 blocks each and one with 6 rows of 16 blocks each. Sew the blocks in each section into rows; press the seam allowances in alternate directions from row to row. Join the rows; press the seam allowances in one direction. Sew the smaller section to the left side of the grid from step 1 and sew the larger section to the top.

3. Arrange the 6½" blocks along the left side and top of the section from step 2. Sew 12 blocks together for the side and 13 blocks together for the top. Sew the rows to the quilt.

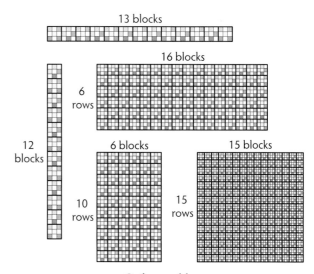

Quilt assembly

Finishing the Quilt

Go to ShopMartingale.com/HowtoQuilt for more details on quilting and finishing.

1. Layer the backing, batting, and quilt top; baste the layers together. Hand or machine quilt as desired. The quilt shown was machine quilted with an allover design.

2. Use the dark-blue 2½"-wide strips to make and attach the binding.

Triple Play

*H*ere's a chance to use precut 10" squares for Nine Patch blocks and block centers. The on-point blocks bring to mind a baseball diamond. The variation in scale and color placement among the blocks makes for a unique and eye-catching quilt.

Materials

Yardage is based on 42"-wide fabric.

1¾ yards of black print for border and binding

⅔ yard of tan print for setting triangles

24 assorted tan-print 10" squares for blocks

22 assorted red-print 10" squares for blocks

20 assorted medium-to-dark print 10" squares (navy, green, gold, purple, black, and pumpkin) for blocks

3½ yards of fabric for backing

63" x 80" piece of batting

Cutting

All measurements include ¼"-wide seam allowances.

From the medium-to-dark print 10" squares, cut:

    120 squares, 2½" x 2½"

    60 squares, 1½" x 1½"

    54 squares, 1" x 1"

From the assorted tan 10" squares, cut:

    24 matching sets of 2 rectangles, 2" x 3½", and 2 rectangles, 2" x 6½"

    264 squares, 1½" x 1½"

    54 squares, 1" x 1"

From the assorted red 10" squares, cut:

    15 matching sets of 2 rectangles, 2" x 3½", and 2 rectangles, 2" x 6½"

    60 squares, 2½" x 2½"

From the tan print, cut:

    5 squares, 9¾" x 9¾"; cut into quarters diagonally to yield 20 triangles

    2 squares, 5⅛" x 5⅛"; cut in half diagonally to yield 4 triangles

From the black print, cut *on the lengthwise grain:*

    4 strips, 6½" x 63"

    5 strips, 2½" x 63"

Triple Play by Kansas Troubles Quilters; designed by Lynne Hagmeier, pieced by Lois Sprecker, and machine quilted by Joy Johnson

Finished quilt: 55" x 72"

Finished block: 6" x 6"

Assembling the Framed 36 Patch Blocks

1. Lay out 18 assorted medium-to-dark and 18 tan 1" squares in six rows of six. Join the squares in each row; press the seam allowances in alternate directions from row to row. Join the rows; press the seam allowances in one direction. Make three.

Make 3.

2. Sew matching red 2" x 3½" rectangles to opposite sides of a 36-patch unit; press the seam allowances toward the red rectangles. Sew matching red 2" x 6½" rectangles to the top and bottom of the unit; press. Repeat to complete all three blocks, which should measure 6½" square.

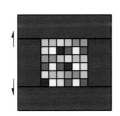

Make 3.

Assembling the Framed Nine Patch Blocks

1. Lay out five assorted medium-to-dark 1½" squares and four assorted tan 1½" squares in three rows of three, alternating the darks and lights. Join the squares in each row; press the seam allowances in opposite directions from row to row. Join the rows; press the seam allowances toward the center.

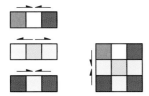

2. Sew matching red 2" x 3½" rectangles to opposite sides of the nine-patch unit; press the seam allowances toward the red rectangles. Sew matching red 2" x 6½" rectangles to the top and bottom of the unit; press. Make 12 red Framed Nine Patch blocks that measure 6½" square.

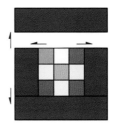

Make 12.

3. Repeat step 1 to assemble a nine-patch unit using nine assorted tan 1½" squares. Repeat step 2 to frame the unit with two matching tan 2" x 3½" rectangles and two matching tan 2" x 6½" rectangles; press. Make 24 tan Framed Nine Patch blocks that measure 6½" square.

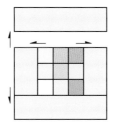

Make 24.

Assembling the Nine Patch Blocks

1. Lay out six assorted medium-to-dark 2½" squares and three assorted red 2½" squares in three rows of three squares each, placing the red squares diagonally across the block as shown. Sew the squares into rows; press the seam allowances in opposite directions from row to row. Sew the rows together to make a Nine Patch block. Press the seam allowances toward the block center. Make 16 blocks that measure 6½" square.

Make 16.

2. Repeat step 1 to make four Nine Patch blocks with the red squares positioned in the center and two corners as shown.

Make 4.

Assembling the Quilt

1. Lay out the blocks on point as shown in the quilt assembly diagram, placing the Framed 36 Patch blocks in the center of the quilt, surrounded by tan Framed Nine Patch blocks, red Framed Nine Patch blocks, and Nine Patch blocks. Rotate the tan-framed blocks so that the seams don't butt up next to the seams in the red-framed blocks. Place the setting triangles along the edges and in the corners.

2. Join the blocks and side setting triangles in diagonal rows; press the seam allowances toward the darker blocks. Join the rows; press the seam

allowances in one direction. Add the corner setting triangles; press the seam allowances toward the corners.

3. Measure the quilt top vertically through the center. (It should measure 59⅞".) Trim two of the black 6½"-wide strips to that measurement. Sew the borders to the sides of the quilt; press the seam allowances toward the borders. Measure the quilt top horizontally through the center, including the borders just added. (It should measure 55".) Cut two strips to that measurement and sew the borders to the top and bottom of the quilt; press.

Finishing the Quilt

Go to ShopMartingale.com/HowtoQuilt for more details on quilting and finishing.

1. Layer the backing, batting, and quilt top; baste the layers together. Hand or machine quilt as desired. The quilt shown was machine quilted in the ditch and has a variety of designs that highlight the shapes in the quilt, including a grid design in the blocks and a triangle design in the border.

2. Use the black 2½"-wide strips to make and attach the binding.

Quilt assembly

Counted Nine Patch

M ake double Nine Patch blocks on the double by building them from smaller nine-patch units. Add pink-and-white cornerstones to create Nine Patch blocks in the sashing for a delightful, unifying touch that gives the quilt the look of counted cross-stitch.

Materials

Yardage is based on 42"-wide fabric. Fat eighths are approximately 9" x 21".

4 yards of white solid for blocks and sashing

12 fat eighths *total* of assorted blue, green, and pink prints for blocks

⅜ yard of pink tone on tone for blocks and sashing

⅔ yard of blue print for binding

5 yards of fabric for backing

68" x 85" piece of batting

Cutting

All measurements include ¼"-wide seam allowances.

From the white solid, cut:

   22 strips, 2" x 42"; crosscut *15 of the strips* into:

      24 rectangles, 2" x 5"

      12 strips, 2" x 21"

      24 strips, 2" x 10"

   6 strips, 5" x 42"; crosscut into 48 squares, 5" x 5"

   4 strips, 14" x 42"; crosscut into 31 strips, 5" x 14"

From *each* of the assorted blue, green, and pink prints, cut:

   2 strips, 2" x 21"

   1 strip, 2" x 10"

From the pink tone on tone, cut:

   5 strips, 2" x 42"

From the blue print, cut:

   8 strips, 2½" x 42"

Counted Nine Patch by Sherri Falls

Finished quilt: 59½" x 77"

Finished block: 13½" x 13½"

Assembling the Blocks

1. Sew a white 2" x 21" strip between two matching print 2" x 21" strips as shown; press the seam allowances toward the print strips. Crosscut the strip set into eight segments, 2" wide.

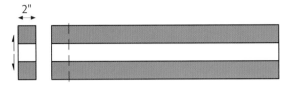

Make 1 strip set.
Cut 8 segments.

2. Using a print that matches the print in step 1, sew a 2" x 10" strip between two white 2" x 10" strips as shown; press the seam allowances toward the print strip. Crosscut the strip set into four segments, 2" wide.

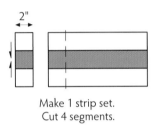

Make 1 strip set.
Cut 4 segments.

3. Arrange two segments from step 1 and one segment from step 2 as shown. Join the segments; press the seam allowances away from the center. Make four identical nine-patch units that measure 5" square.

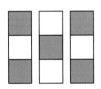

Make 4.

4. Repeat steps 1–3 with the remaining print strips to make a total of 48 nine-patch units.

5. Sew a white 2" x 42" strip between two pink 2" x 42" strips as shown; press the seam allowances toward the pink strips. Crosscut the strip set into 20 segments, 2" wide.

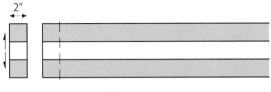

Make 1 strip set.
Cut 20 segments.

6. Sew a pink 2" x 42" strip between two white 2" x 42" strips as shown; press the seam allowances toward the pink strip. Make three strip sets. From the strip sets, cut 52 segments, 2" wide.

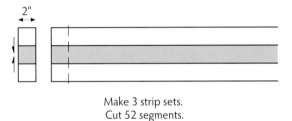

Make 3 strip sets.
Cut 52 segments.

7. Join one segment from step 5 and two segments from step 6 to make a sashing block as shown. Make 20 sashing blocks that measure 5" square.

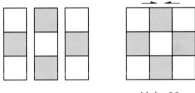

Make 20.

8. Sew one of the remaining segments from step 6 between two white 2" x 5" rectangles as shown to make a block center; press the seam allowances toward the white rectangles. Make 12 units that measure 5" square.

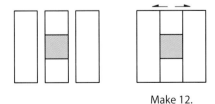

Make 12.

9. Arrange four white 5" squares, four matching nine-patch units, and one block center in three rows as shown. Join the units in each row; press the seam allowances as indicated by the arrows. Join the rows; press the seam allowances away from the center. Make one block from each print for a total of 12 blocks.

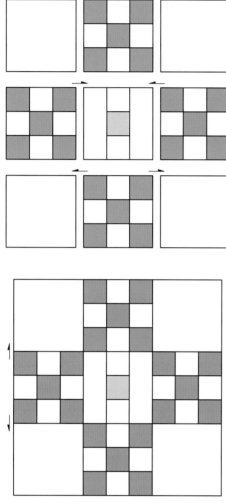

Make 12.

Assembling the Quilt

1. Arrange three blocks and four white 5" x 14" sashing strips in a row as shown. Join the blocks and strips; press the seam allowances toward the sashing strips. Make four rows.

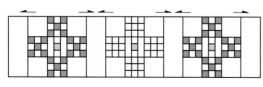

Make 4.

2. Join three white 5" x 14" sashing strips and four sashing blocks as shown; press the seam allowances toward the sashing strips. Make five sashing rows.

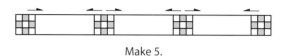

Make 5.

3. Lay out the block and sashing rows as shown in the quilt assembly diagram. Join the rows; press the seam allowances toward the sashing rows.

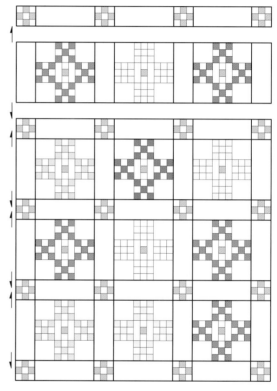

Quilt assembly

Finishing the Quilt

Go to ShopMartingale.com/HowtoQuilt for more details on quilting and finishing.

1. Layer the backing, batting, and quilt top; baste the layers together. Hand or machine quilt as desired. The quilt shown was machine quilted with an allover swirl design.

2. Use the blue 2½"-wide strips to make and attach the binding.

Paisley Patch

Bold Nine Patch and Snowball blocks combine to make a cheerful and dynamic composition. The on-point setting and color-coordinated arrangement adds extra interest to the quick and easy patchwork. Incorporate red, cream, and blue paisley prints for a classic look.

Materials

Yardage is based on 42"-wide fabric. Fat eighths are approximately 9" x 21".

1⅝ yards *total* of assorted light prints for blocks

1⅓ yards of light print for setting triangles and inner border

10 fat eighths of assorted red prints for blocks

10 fat eighths of assorted blue prints for blocks

1 yard of blue print for outer border

⅔ yard of dark-blue print for binding

4⅔ yards of fabric for backing

72" x 84" piece of batting

Cutting

All measurements include ¼"-wide seam allowances.

From *each* of the assorted red and blue prints, cut:*

    1 strip, 4" x 21"; crosscut into:

        2 squares, 4" x 4"

        3 squares, 3½" x 3½"

    1 strip, 3½" x 21"; crosscut into:

        1 rectangle, 3½" x 7½"

        3 squares, 3½" x 3½"

From the assorted light prints, cut:

    20 matching sets of 2 rectangles, 3½" x 7½", and 1 square, 3½" x 3½"

    12 matching sets of 2 squares, 4" x 4", and 1 square, 3½" x 3½"

From the light print, cut:

    6 strips, 2½" x 42"

    4 squares, 14" x 14"; cut into quarters diagonally to yield 16 triangles (2 are extra)

    2 squares, 7¼" x 7¼"; cut in half diagonally to yield 4 triangles

From the blue print, cut:

    7 strips, 4½" x 42"

From the dark-blue print, cut:

    8 strips, 2½" x 42"

*Keep like fabric pieces of the same size together for easier block assembly.

Paisley Patch, designed and pieced by Sherri McConnell; quilted by Abby Latimer

Finished quilt: 63½" x 76"

Finished block: 9" x 9"

Assembling the Nine Patch Blocks

1. Sew one print 3½" x 7½" rectangle between two matching light 3½" x 7½" rectangles as shown to make a short strip set. Press the seam allowances toward the print rectangle. Crosscut the strip set into two segments, 3½" wide.

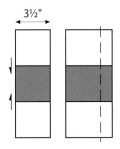

Make 1 strip set.
Cut 2 segments.

2. Using light and print fabrics that match those in step 1, sew a light 3½" square and two print 3½" squares together as shown. Press the seam allowances toward the print squares.

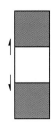

3. Join the units from steps 1 and 2 as shown to complete the Nine Patch block. Press the seam allowances open.

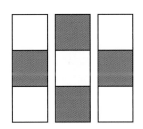 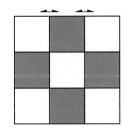

4. Repeat steps 1–3 to make a total of 10 red blocks and 10 blue blocks that measure 9½" square.

Assembling the Snowball Blocks

1. Draw a diagonal line from corner to corner on the wrong side of two matching light 4" squares. With right sides together, place the marked squares on two matching print 4" squares. Sew ¼" from each side of the drawn line. Cut the units apart on the drawn line to yield four matching half-square-triangle units. Press the seam allowances open. Trim each unit to 3½" square.

Make 4.

2. Lay out the four half-square-triangle units, four matching print 3½" squares, and one matching light 3½" square in three rows as shown. Join the units in each row; press the seam allowances in alternating directions. Join the rows; press the seam allowances open.

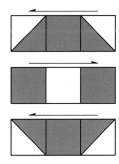 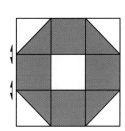

3. Repeat steps 1 and 2 to make a total of six blue blocks and six red blocks that measure 9½" square. **Note:** You will have 8 extra 4" squares and 16 extra 3½" squares.

Assembling the Quilt

1. Lay out the blocks, setting them on point and alternating the Nine Patch and Snowball blocks and also alternating the colors as shown in the quilt assembly diagram below. Place the side setting triangles along the edges, and place the corner triangles in the corners.

2. Join the blocks and side setting triangles in diagonal rows; press the seam allowances in opposite directions from row to row. Join the rows; press the seam allowances in one direction. It's easiest to join the top four rows and then the bottom four rows and then join the two sections. Sew the corner triangles last; press the seam allowances toward the corners.

3. To make the inner border, piece the light 2½"-wide strips end to end. Measure the quilt top vertically through the center. (It should measure 61½" long.) From the total length, cut two strips to that measurement for the side borders. Sew the borders to the sides of the quilt; press the seam allowances toward the borders. Measure the quilt horizontally through the center, including the borders just added. (It should measure 53½" wide.) Cut two strips to that measurement and sew the borders to the top and bottom of the quilt; press.

4. Piece the blue 4½"-wide strips end to end. Repeat the procedure in step 3 to measure, cut, and add the side borders and then the top and bottom borders.

Finishing the Quilt

Go to ShopMartingale.com/HowtoQuilt for more details on quilting and finishing.

1. Layer the backing, batting, and quilt top; baste the layers together. Hand or machine quilt as desired. The quilt shown was machine quilted with an allover wave pattern.

2. Use the dark-blue 2½"-wide strips to make and attach the binding.

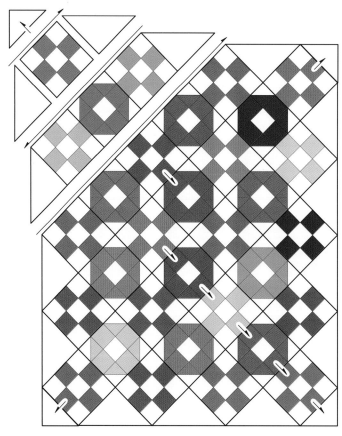

Quilt assembly

Wash-Day Blues

The soft shades of blue and lavender in this quilt are reminiscent of blue jeans and chambray shirts blowing in the breeze on an outdoor wash line. But this scrappy little Nine Patch design would be just as much fun and as quick to make using your own favorite color palette.

Materials

Yardage is based on 42"-wide fabric.

½ yard of dusty-aqua solid for outer border

⅜ yard *total* of scraps or 1½"-wide strips of assorted blues, grays, and purples for blocks

¼ yard of navy solid for inner border

¼ yard of orchid solid for setting squares

¼ yard of periwinkle solid for setting triangles

¼ yard of dusty-teal solid for binding

1 yard of fabric for backing

32" x 36" piece of batting

Fabric Options

Karen used hand-dyed solids to give a soft, mottled look to her quilt. If you like the look but don't have access to hand-dyed fabrics, you can use commercial solids, which are available in dozens of shades, or consider using shot cottons. These fabrics are woven from two different-colored solid threads—one for the warp and one for the weft—giving them an unusual but interesting glow.

Cutting

All measurements include ¼"-wide seam allowances.

For Each Block (Cut 20 blocks total.)

From the scraps of assorted blues, grays, and purples, cut:*

5 matching dark squares, 1½" x 1½"

4 matching light squares, 1½" x 1½"

For the Remainder of the Quilt

From the orchid solid, cut:

12 squares, 3½" x 3½"

Most of the blocks have 5 dark and 4 light squares, but in a few, the values are swapped (5 light and 4 dark). You can also substitute a few of the matching squares in the blocks with random squares for a scrappier make-do look, as in the quilt shown.

Continued on page 63

Wash-Day Blues by Karen Costello Soltys
Finished quilt: 25½" x 29¾"
Finished block: 3" x 3"

Continued from page 61

From the periwinkle solid, cut:

   4 squares, 5½" x 5½"; cut into quarters diagonally to yield 16 triangles (2 are extra)

   2 squares, 3" x 3"; cut in half diagonally to yield 4 triangles

From the navy solid, cut:

   3 strips, 1½" x 42"; crosscut into:

      2 strips, 1½" x 19½"

      2 strips, 1½" x 21¾"

From the dusty-aqua solid, cut:

   4 strips, 3½" x 42"; crosscut into:

      2 strips, 3½" x 23¾"

      2 strips, 3½" x 25½"

From the dusty-teal solid, cut:

   3 strips, 2" x 42"**

**Karen prefers a narrower binding on small quilts; cut wider strips if you prefer.

Assembling the Blocks

To achieve a scrappy look, these blocks are made from individual squares, rather than strip pieced. Choose one dark and one light fabric for each block, or mix in some different ones for interest.

1. Lay out the pieces for one block, alternating the dark and light colors as shown.

2. Join the squares in rows and press the seam allowances toward the darker fabrics. Join the rows; press the seam allowances away from the center. (See "Chain Piecing Individual Squares" on page 6.)

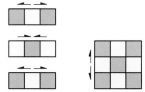

3. Repeat steps 1 and 2 to make 20 Nine Patch blocks that measure 3½" square.

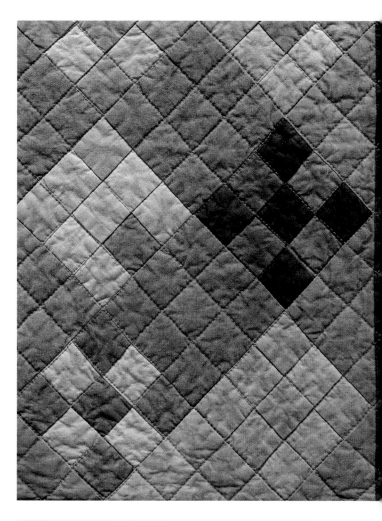

Chain-Piecing Option

If you wish, you can lay out several or all 20 blocks at once and chain piece the squares to sew more than one block at a time. To chain piece, sew the pieces from each block together one after the other without cutting the thread in between. For more on this, see "Chain Piecing Individual Squares" on page 6.

Assembling the Quilt

1. Using a design wall, floor, or other large flat surface, lay out the Nine Patch blocks and orchid 3½" squares in diagonal rows, referring to the quilt assembly diagram below. Place the periwinkle quarter-square triangles along the outer edges. Place the four half-square triangles in the corners.

2. Rearrange the blocks until you're pleased with the layout. Join the blocks and side triangles in diagonal rows. Press the seam allowances toward the unpieced squares and triangles.

3. Join the rows and press the seam allowances in one direction; add the corner triangles and press the seam allowances toward the corners.

4. Sew the navy 1½" x 21¾" strips to the sides of the quilt top. Press the seam allowances toward the navy strips. Sew the navy 1½" x 19½" strips to the top and bottom of the quilt; press.

5. Sew the dusty-aqua 3½" x 23¾" strips to the sides of the quilt top; press the seam allowances toward the dusty-aqua strips. Sew the dusty-aqua 3½" x 25½" strips to the top and bottom; press.

Finishing the Quilt

Go to ShopMartingale.com/HowtoQuilt for more details on quilting and finishing.

1. Mark any quilting motifs desired, and then layer the backing, batting, and quilt top; baste the layers together. Hand or machine quilt as desired. The quilt shown is machine quilted in a straight-line grid, using the seamlines of the Nine Patch blocks as a guide.

2. Use the dusty-teal 2"-wide strips to make and attach the binding.

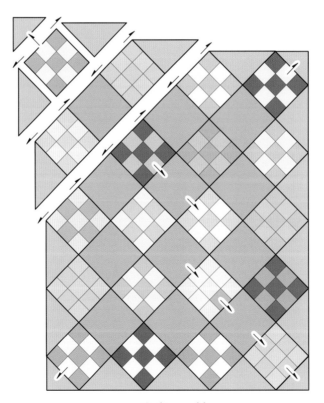

Quilt assembly

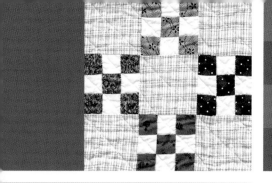

Old Nine

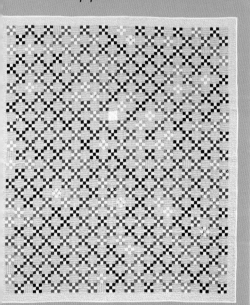

Materials

Yardage is based on 42"-wide fabric.

3⅓ yards *total* of assorted dark prints for blocks*

3⅓ yards of light check or plaid for setting blocks

2⅝ yards *total* of assorted cream prints for blocks*

2⅝ yards of light stripe for border

¾ yard of light print for binding

7¼ yards of fabric for backing

86" x 98" piece of batting

You can use leftover 1½"-wide strips, precut 5" squares, and other scraps from your stash. If using precut strips, you'll need a cream 1½" x 7" strip and a dark-print 1½" x 9" strip for each Nine Patch block.

Cutting

All measurements include ¼"-wide seam allowances.

From the assorted cream prints, cut:

336 matching sets of 1 rectangle, 1½" x 5", and 1 square, 1½" x 1½"

From the assorted dark prints, cut:

336 matching sets of 1 rectangle, 1½" x 5", and 1 rectangle, 1½" x 3½"

From the light check or plaid, cut:

28 strips, 3½" x 42"; crosscut into 336 squares, 3½" x 3½"

From the light stripe, cut *on the lengthwise grain:*

4 strips, 3½" x 90"*

From the light print, cut:

9 strips, 2½" x 42"

Use the remainder of the fabric to make a pieced backing if desired.

Scrap Saver

After finishing a quilt, cut little scraps into 1½", 2½", and 4½" strips. Sweep them into a bin and save them for projects just like this one.

Assembling the Blocks

1. Select a cream 1½" x 5" rectangle, a matching cream 1½" square, one dark 1½" x 5" rectangle, and a matching dark 1½" x 3½" rectangle for one block.

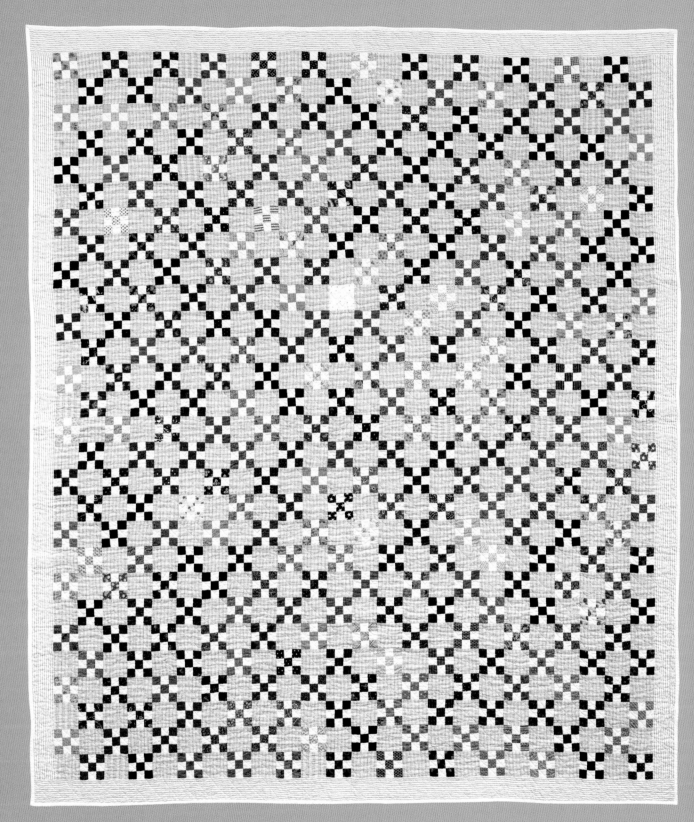

Old Nine by Tammy Vonderschmitt
Finished quilt: 78½" x 90½"
Finished block: 3" x 3"

2. Join the square and rectangles as shown; press the seam allowances toward the dark rectangles. Clip into the seam allowances next to the square so that the dark rectangle will lie flat.

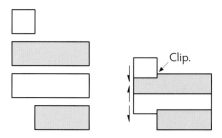

3. Cut the pieced unit into 1½"-wide segments as shown. Cut the segment with the square on the left side first. Then straighten the right edge, rotate the piece 180°, and cut the two remaining segments.

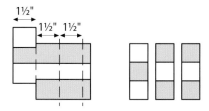

4. Arrange the three segments as shown. Sew the segments together; press the seam allowances away from the center.

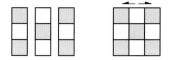

5. Repeat steps 1–4 to make a total of 336 blocks that measure 3½" square.

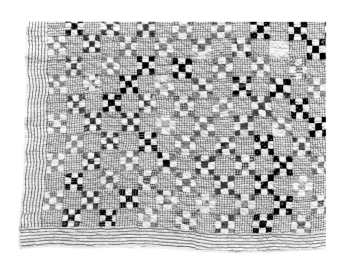

Here is a portion of the antique quilt that inspired Old Nine.

Assembling the Quilt

1. Arrange 28 rows with 12 Nine Patch blocks and 12 light check or plaid 3½" squares in each. Alternate the blocks and squares as shown. Join the blocks and squares in pairs, and then join the pairs; press the seam allowances toward the light squares. Join the rows; press the seam allowances in one direction.

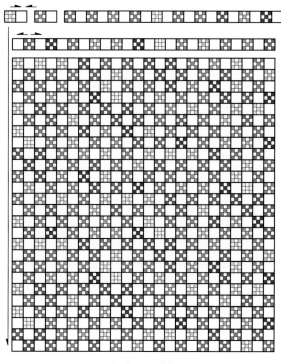

Quilt assembly

2. Measure the quilt top vertically through the center. (It should measure 72½" x 84½".) From the light stripe, cut two pieces to that measurement for the side borders. Sew the borders to the sides of the quilt; press the seam allowances toward the borders. Repeat to measure, cut, and sew the top and bottom borders.

Finishing the Quilt

Go to ShopMartingale.com/HowtoQuilt for more details on quilting and finishing.

1. Layer the backing, batting, and quilt top; baste the layers together. Hand or machine quilt as desired. The quilt shown was machine quilted in diagonal parallel lines like the antique inspiration quilt.

2. Use the light-print 2½"-wide strips to make and attach the binding.

Patches and Pomegranates, designed, pieced, and appliquéd by Debbie Roberts; custom machine quilted by Linda Hrcka, The Quilted Pineapple

Finished quilt: 47" x 47"

Finished block: 3" x 3"

Patches and Pomegranates

Patchwork and appliqué go together like peas and carrots, to paraphrase Forrest Gump. Frame a lovely appliqué bouquet of pomegranates and berries with colorful Nine Patch blocks set on point.

Materials

Yardage is based on 42"-wide fabric.

1 yard *total* of assorted dark prints for blocks

1 yard *total* of assorted light prints for blocks

1 yard of medium print for alternate blocks

⅞ yard of dark-brown print for appliqué backgrounds, center-block border, and setting triangles

Scraps of assorted colorful prints or solids for appliqué

½ yard of red print for binding

3⅛ yards of fabric for backing

55" x 55" piece of batting

¼" bias-tape maker

Cutting

All measurements include ¼"-wide seam allowances.

From the scraps of assorted colorful prints or solids, cut *on the bias* for the appliqué stems:

    1 strip, ½" x 4½"

    1 strip, ½" x 5½"

    1 strip, ½" x 9"

    1 strip, ½" x 9½"

    2 strips, ½" x 6"

    8 strips, ½" x 8" (for corner triangles)

From the dark-brown print, cut:

    1 strip, 13½" x 42"; crosscut into:

        1 square, 13½" x 13½"

        2 squares, 12½" x 12½"; cut in half diagonally to yield 4 corner triangles

    3 squares, 4¼" x 4¼"

    4 squares, 2½" x 2½"

    1 strip, 6" x 42"; crosscut into 6 squares, 6" x 6". Cut into quarters diagonally to yield 24 side triangles.

Continued on page 70

Continued from page 69

From the assorted light prints, cut:

4 squares, 2½" x 2½"

12 squares, 2⅜" x 2⅜"

4 squares, 2" x 2"

384 squares*, 1½" x 1½"

From the assorted dark prints, cut:

480 squares*, 1½" x 1½"

From the medium print, cut:

8 strips, 3½" x 42"; crosscut into 84 squares,
3½" x 3½"

From the red print, cut:

5 strips, 2½" x 42"

*If you want the fabrics to match within a block, cut the
light prints in matching sets of 4 squares and the dark
prints in matching sets of 5 squares.*

Adding the Appliqué

1. Prepare the appliqués from assorted scraps using
the patterns on page 75. Use the appliqué method
of your choice.

2. Use the bias-tape maker to prepare the bias stems
using the ½"-wide bias strips.

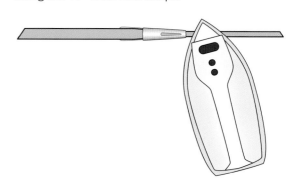

Center square appliqué placement

3. Position and appliqué the pieces to the 13½" center square using your favorite method and referring to the placement guide on page 70. In the diagram the B label stands for berry, L for leaf, F for flower center, and S for seed. When the appliqué is complete, trim the center square to 12½" x 12½", keeping the appliqué centered.

4. Fold a corner triangle in half to make a crease in the center. Position and appliqué the stems, leaves, and berries as shown in the placement guide below. Repeat with each corner triangle. The triangles are cut slightly oversized and will be trimmed later after the quilt top is completed.

Assembling the Quilt Center

1. Draw a diagonal line from corner to corner on the wrong side of the light-print 2½" squares. With right sides together, pair a marked light-print square with a dark-brown 2½" square. Sew a scant ¼" from each side of the drawn line. Cut along the diagonal line to make two half-square-triangle units. Press the seam allowances toward the dark-brown print. Make a total of eight units that measure 2" square.

Make 8.

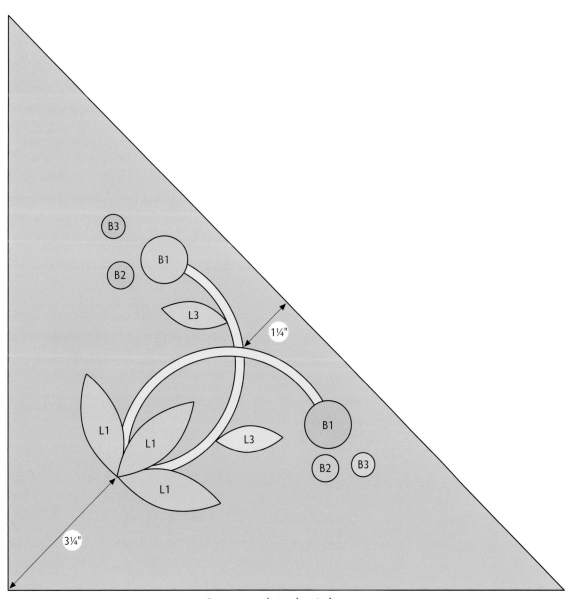

Corner triangle appliqué placement

2. Draw a diagonal line on the wrong side of each light-print 2⅜" square. Align two of the marked light-print squares on opposite corners of each dark-brown 4¼" square. Stitch a scant ¼" from each side of the drawn lines. Cut apart on the drawn lines and press the seam allowances toward the small triangles.

3. Place a marked light-print square from step 2 on each of the cut pieces and stitch a scant ¼" from each side of the drawn line. Cut along the drawn line and press the seam allowances toward the light triangle. Trim the dog-ears. The flying-geese unit should measure 2" x 3½". Make a total of 12 flying-geese units.

Make 12.

4. Stitch together three flying-geese units and two half-square-triangle units. Press the seam allowances as shown. Make four border rows. Sew a light-print 2" square to each end of two of the borders. Press the seam allowances toward the light-print squares.

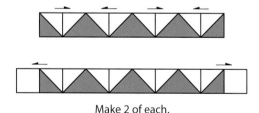

Make 2 of each.

5. Sew the shorter borders to the sides of the appliquéd center block. Press the seam allowances toward the appliquéd block. Sew the remaining two borders to the top and bottom of the appliquéd center block; press.

Assembling the Nine Patch Blocks

1. Select four light-print 1½" squares and five dark-print 1½" squares for one block. Use matching fabrics, or make it scrappy and mix them up!

2. Arrange the squares as shown and sew them into three rows. Press the seam allowances as shown, or refer to "Clipping Trick" on page 73 to press all the seam allowances toward the dark-print squares. Sew the rows together and press. The block should measure 3½" square.

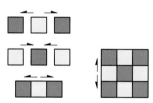

3. Repeat steps 1 and 2 to make a total of 96 blocks.

Clipping Trick

Clip through both layers of the seam allowance, up to the seamline, ¼" from each side of the seam intersection as shown. Press the seam allowances toward the dark fabric. Press the center of the intersection open.

 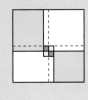

Clip.

Assembling the Quilt Top

1. Arrange and sew the Nine Patch blocks and medium-print 3½"-square alternate blocks into rows, starting and ending each row with a Nine Patch block. Press the seam allowances toward the alternate blocks. Make the following:
   - 2 rows of 8 Nine Patch blocks and 7 alternate blocks
   - 2 rows of 7 Nine Patch blocks and 6 alternate blocks
   - 2 rows of 6 Nine Patch blocks and 5 alternate blocks
   - 2 rows of 5 Nine Patch blocks and 4 alternate blocks
   - 2 rows of 4 Nine Patch blocks and 3 alternate blocks
   - 2 rows of 3 Nine Patch blocks and 2 alternate blocks

2. Arrange one row of each length together with the side setting triangles and one of the appliquéd corner triangles as shown. Sew the side triangles to the rows, aligning the right angle of the triangles with the block corners; press the seam allowances toward the triangles. Sew the rows together and add the corner triangle to make a side section. The side and corner setting triangles were cut oversized and will be trimmed later. Press the seam allowances in one direction. Make two side sections.

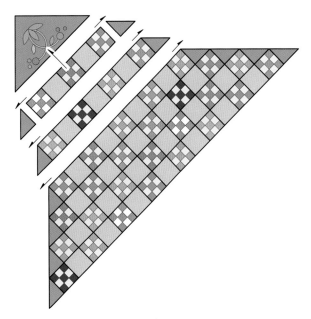

Make 2.

3. Arrange and sew three Nine Patch blocks and three alternate blocks together to make a row as shown. Press the seam allowances toward the alternate blocks. Make 10 rows.

Make 10.

4. Sew five of the rows from step 3 together as shown. Press the seam allowances as indicated. Make two end sections.

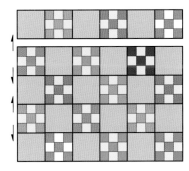

Make 2.

5. Stitch the end sections to opposite sides of the appliquéd center block. Press the seam allowances toward the end sections. Add an appliquéd corner triangle to each end. Press the seam allowances toward the triangles.

6. Stitch the side sections to the center appliquéd section. Press the seam allowances toward the side sections. Trim and square up the quilt top, leaving a ¼" seam allowance outside the points of the Nine Patch blocks.

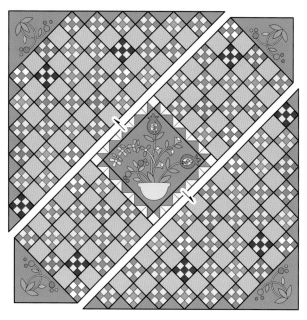

Quilt assembly

Finishing the Quilt

Go to ShopMartingale.com/HowtoQuilt for more details on quilting and finishing.

1. Layer the backing, batting, and quilt top; baste the layers together. Hand or machine quilt as desired. The quilt shown was machine quilted with a central feather motif, curved grid work, echoing curves in the alternate blocks, and curves and a grid in each Nine Patch block.

2. Use the red 2½"-wide strips to make and attach the binding.

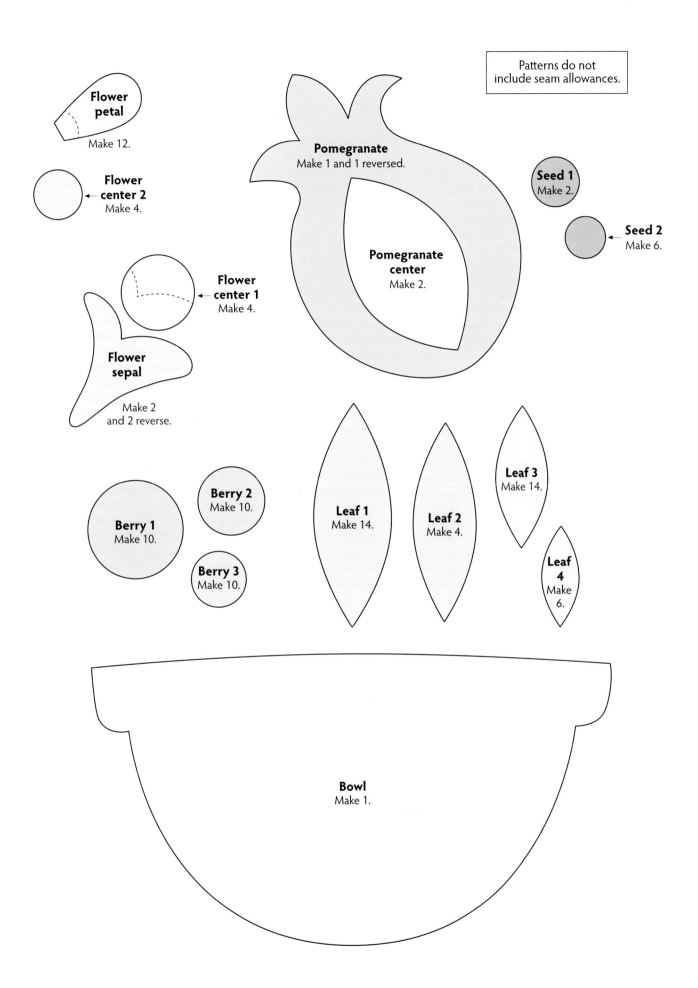

Patterns do not include seam allowances.

Flower petal
Make 12.

Flower center 2
Make 4.

Flower center 1
Make 4.

Flower sepal
Make 2 and 2 reverse.

Pomegranate
Make 1 and 1 reversed.

Pomegranate center
Make 2.

Seed 1
Make 2.

Seed 2
Make 6.

Berry 1
Make 10.

Berry 2
Make 10.

Berry 3
Make 10.

Leaf 1
Make 14.

Leaf 2
Make 4.

Leaf 3
Make 14.

Leaf 4
Make 6.

Bowl
Make 1.

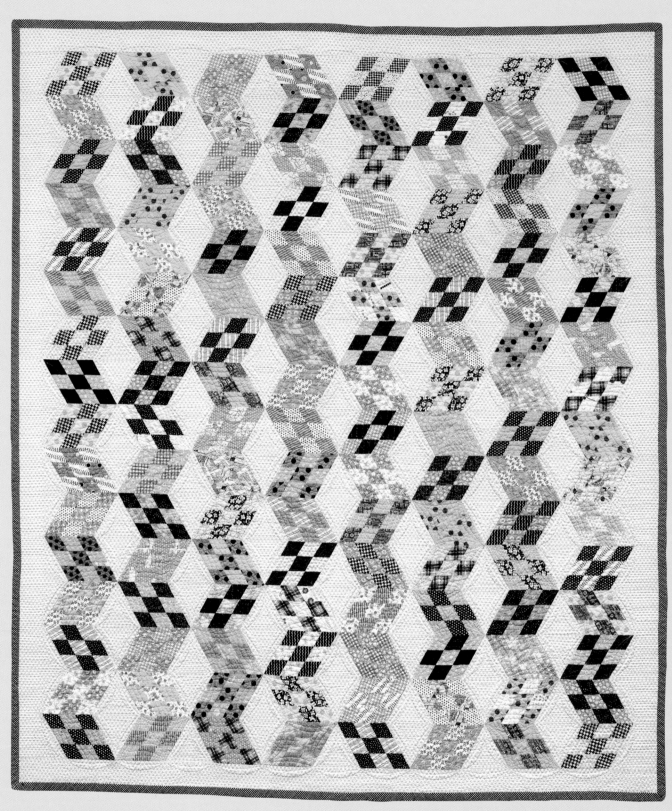

Tilt by Carrie Nelson
Finished quilt: 68½" x 78"
Finished 60° diamond: 4½"

Tilt

Give a simple Nine Patch block a little push, and you have a Diamond Nine Patch! This fabulous quilt may look complex, but it's really quite easy to piece—and it will provide an outlet for many of those orphan scraps yearning for a forever home.

Materials

Yardage is based on 42"-wide fabric. Fat quarters are approximately 18" x 21".

26 fat quarters of assorted light, medium, and dark prints for blocks

2¼ yards of light print for background

⅞ yard of small-scale black-and-white plaid for binding

4⅞ yards of fabric for backing

76" x 86" piece of batting

Ruler with 60° angle lines

Cutting

All measurements include ¼"-wide seam allowances.

From the light print, cut:

13 strips, 5" x 42"

4 strips, 3" x 42"

From the assorted light, medium, and dark prints, cut:

128 sets of 3 matching strips, 2" x 10½"

From the small-scale black-and-white plaid, cut:

3"-wide bias strips to total 306"*

*The quilt shown features an extra-wide, single-fold binding. Cut narrower strips if you prefer a narrower binding.

Cutting the Background Pieces

The Nine Patch blocks are 60° diamonds, so the background pieces must be cut to fit. The background is composed of 112 triangles to fit between the blocks and 32 trapezoids for the ends of the rows. Cut the triangles and end pieces from the light-print 5" x 42" strips according to the instructions that follow on page 78.

1. Fold a light-print 5" x 42" strip in half lengthwise, wrong sides together. Measure 3" from the left end along the top edge and approximately 6" from the left end along the bottom edge of the strip. Placing your ruler at these measurements, align the 60° line of the ruler with the top edge of the strip and make the first cut. To make the second cut, rotate the ruler in the opposite direction, ¼" to the right. You will be cutting a triangle with a ¼"-wide flat top. (If you have a 60° triangle ruler, you can cut with that instead.) Continue moving across the strip to cut five layered pairs of triangles. Open the

fold and cut one additional triangle. Save the strip ends for the next step. Cut 11 of the strips in this manner to yield 112 triangles.

Note that cutting with two layers of fabric wrong sides together will give you a pair of end pieces, one of which will be reversed.

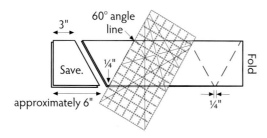

Cut 112 triangles.

2. Fold the two remaining light-print 5" x 42" strips in half lengthwise, wrong sides together. Cut pieces with one 60° angle and one right angle as shown, with short sides that measure 3". Use the leftover pieces from step 2 as needed to cut a total of 16 end pieces and 16 reversed end pieces.

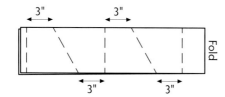

Cut 16 end pieces and 16 reversed end pieces.

Assembling the Diamond Nine Patch Blocks

1. Choose two sets of three matching 2" x 10½" strips. Make two strip sets as shown, offsetting each strip by 1". Press the seam allowances open.

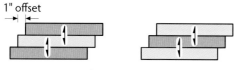

Make 2 strip sets.

2. Using the 60° line of the ruler, trim the left side of the strip set as shown. Cut three segments, 2" wide, from each strip set. Note that you may be

able to cut a fourth segment if you're careful. Use those bonus segments to make a pieced backing, or save them for another project.

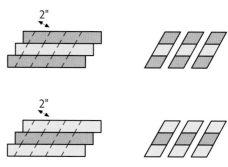

Cut 3 segments from each.

3. Arrange and sew the segments together as shown. Press the seam allowances open. Make two Diamond Nine Patch blocks.

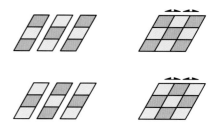

4. Repeat steps 1–3 to make a total of 128 blocks.

Finding the Sweet Spot

When you sew the segments together, they will be slightly offset. The seam should start and end at the V.

If you've cut and stitched your seams accurately and consistently, the seams will line up perfectly, or nearly perfectly, 99% of the time—without pins! With the seam allowances pressed open, here's how to find the sweet spot: the edge of each seam allowance should almost touch the seamline of the next segment.

Assembling the Quilt

1. Arrange the blocks in 16 rows with eight blocks, seven triangles, and two end pieces in each, as shown below. Sew the blocks and triangles into rows and press the seam allowances in opposite directions from row to row.

2. Sew the rows together and press the seam allowances open or in one direction. The end pieces will create what appears to be a side border. Stay stitch the sides ⅛" from the edges to prevent the seams from separating during basting and quilting.

3. Piece the four light-print 3" x 42" strips together using a diagonal seam. Measure the width of your quilt through the center and cut two strips to that measurement.

4. Sew the border strips to the top and bottom of the quilt. Press the seam allowances toward the borders.

Finishing the Quilt

Go to ShopMartingale.com/HowtoQuilt for more details on quilting and finishing.

1. Layer the backing, batting, and quilt top; baste the layers together. Hand or machine quilt as desired.

The quilt shown was machine quilted with echoing arcs and back-and-forth curved lines in the background shapes.

2. Use the plaid 3"-wide bias strips to make and attach the binding, referring to "Single-Fold Binding Option" below.

Single-Fold Binding Option

Carrie wanted an extra-wide binding on her quilt, so she cut bias strips 3" wide. If you want a similar look, join the bias strips to make one long length and sew them to the quilt using a ¾" seam allowance. Fold the binding to the back of the quilt, turn under the raw edge so that it covers the machine stitching, and stitch it to the backing using a blind stitch. Carrie notes that a single-fold binding is probably not advisable for quilts that will be used and washed a lot, because it will wear out more quickly. But it looks great and she won't mind replacing it, if and when it needs replacing.

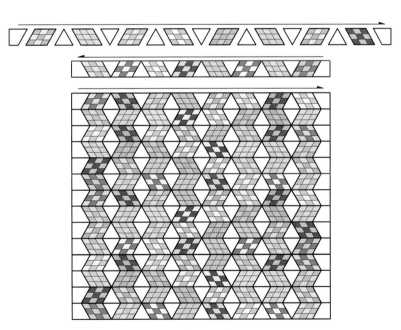

Quilt assembly

About the Contributors

Susan Ache
Having always loved handwork and embroidery, Susan thought to try something new by making a quilt for her mother. When her quilting obsession began, Susan had five children and a supportive husband all running through the house. Now, with five grown children out of the house and one grown husband still by her side, she designs and creates quilts using everyday life as her inspiration and fabric as her playground.

Audrie Bidwell
Born in Singapore and raised in Australia, Audrie started sewing when she moved to the United States, and found her passion in quilting. Audrie loves working with bright colors and drawing inspiration from traditional designs. She lives in Connecticut with her husband. You can find her at blueisbleu.blogspot.com.

Kari M. Carr
A proud member of the Creative Grids Ruler design team and a BERNINA ambassador, Kari owns New Leaf Stitches, a pattern-design company, and created the innovative notion Clearly Perfect Angles. This "recycled Home Ec teacher," quilting instructor, and author is pleased to have cohosted PBS television's *Love of Quilting*. Visit newleafstitches.com.

Barb Cherniwchan
Barb retired from the practice of law to be at home with her growing family. As the kids got older, Barb began a new career in quilting, starting with an online quilt shop, then two brick-and-mortar stores, then a wholesale-pattern partnership, then designing quilt patterns. You can visit her at coachhousedesigns.com.

Sherri Falls
A quilter since 1994, Sherri is the owner of This & That Pattern Company. In 2000, Sherri started a machine-quilting business with her mother, who owns a quilt store in scenic Waconia, Minnesota. You can visit Sherri at thisandthatpatterns.com.

Lynne Hagmeier
A passion for vintage quilts inspired Lynne to take her first quilting class in 1987. Working in a quilt shop and stitching small quilts to sell led to selling patterns for the quilts she designed. Lynne has been designing popular fabric lines for Moda for 15 years.

Kimberly Jolly
Kimberly owns Fat Quarter Shop, an online fabric store, and It's Sew Emma, a pattern company. She has been quilting for more than 15 years. Her designs are often inspired by vintage quilts and blocks, but she occasionally ventures out to try something new. She loves to create quilts for friends and family, especially her children, who are a constant source of inspiration.

Sherri McConnell
Sherri received her first sewing machine when she was about 10 and has been sewing clothing and home-decor items ever since. After receiving a "gentle push" from her grandmother, she branched out into quilting and hasn't stopped. You can visit Sherri at aquiltinglife.com.

Carrie Nelson
After 12 years running Miss Rosie's Quilt Company, Carrie got herself a traditional full-time job working at Moda Fabrics. Among Carrie's books devoted to making quilts from 5" or 10" squares are *Schnibbles Times Two* and *Another Bite of Schnibbles*. You can find Carrie online at blog.modafabrics.com.

Kari Ramsay
The owner of Fresh Cut Quilts Pattern Co., Kari has designed fabric for Henry Glass & Co. and has had her patterns featured in numerous magazines and books. She loves to make quilting easier and more fun for everyone. You can find her at freshcutquilts.com.

Debbie Roberts
Debbie owns the Quilted Moose, a thriving shop in Gretna, Nebraska, where she shares her passion for fabric and quiting. Visit her at quiltedmoose.com.

Karen Costello Soltys
Karen is a knitting, rug-hooking, quilting, movie-watching, reading, and backyard chicken-raising enthusiast. When not pursuing those interests, she works at Martingale as its content director. Karen is the author of *Bits and Pieces* and has designed projects for numerous other books, including *Hooked on Wool*, *A Baker's Dozen*, and *Jelly Babies*.

Tammy Vonderschmitt
Wanting more time to spend with her children, Tammy quit her engineering job and bought a quilt shop. While she'd always sewn, she'd never made a quilt. So she hired a teacher and took her first quilt class along with her customers. Tammy had her shop, Needle in the Haystack, for 11 years and now works for Moda Fabrics.

Jackie White
A quilt teacher, lecturer, and pattern designer, Jackie has a passion for creating three-dimensional art quilts. Her patterns have been published in several books and magazines. She loves embellishing so much that half her studio is devoted to embellishments. You can find her online at jabotquilt.blogspot.com.

Corey Yoder
A quilty mom of two girls and wife to one great husband, Corey enjoys playing with fabric in the form of quilts and quilt design. You can find her at corianderquilts.com.